CONTENTS

Cover design by Wendy Dunbar
Printed by W & G Baird Ltd.

NORTHERN IRELAND AND CANADA

A guide to Northern Ireland sources for the study
of Canadian history, c.1705-1992

© 1994 QUB, PRONI

Compiled and edited by Stephen Davison B.A.,
on behalf of the Centre of Canadian Studies, The Queen's University of
Belfast, and the Public Record Office of Northern Ireland

Cover illustration: *'Curling in Canada', depicting Lord Dufferin as
Governor General of Canada (1872-9). Copied by kind
permission of the Marchioness of Dufferin and Ava,
Patron of the Centre of Canadian Studies, The Queen's
University of Belfast.*

ISBN 0-905691-33-4

FOREWORD

The Centre of Canadian Studies, The Queen's University of Belfast

The Centre, one of five in the United Kingdom, has existed formally since 1986. With generous assistance from the Canadian High Commission in London, it co-ordinates an active programme of teaching and research across the various disciplines at Queen's. In addition, it organizes regular conferences, seminars and lectures by visiting speakers. It is supported by administrative and library services provided by the University.

The Public Record Office of Northern Ireland

Since its creation in 1923, the Public Record Office of Northern Ireland (PRONI), has acted as repository for records pertaining to Northern Ireland's archival heritage. PRONI encourages the widest possible use of its resources, placing emphasis where possible on collaboration with other institutions, so that a whole array of historical sources, archival and artefacts, can be seen in relation to each other. Hence PRONI's enthusiastic support for this joint project, and co-operation with the project researcher, Stephen Davison, whose diligent examination of sources forms the basis of this publication.

PRONI is pleased to be associated with the publication of *Northern Ireland and Canada*, and expresses the hope that it will benefit researchers on both sides of the Atlantic.

INTRODUCTION

When I began work on this catalogue, the principal objective was to produce a comprehensive survey of the historical material with a Canadian interest which was available in Northern Ireland. It was hoped that this survey would highlight the extent of the connections which exist between Ulster and Canada. This hope has not been disappointed.

From an Ulster perspective, almost every town and village is referred to in the entries as having had some relationship with the other side of the Atlantic. Individuals and families have been touched by the effects of emigration and those who travelled often took with them ideas and aspirations which led to more formal political and religious links being fostered alongside their personal ambitions in Canada.

On the Canadian side, there is ample evidence displayed here to demonstrate the effects such Ulster men and women have had on the development of that country. Settlers of Ulster stock have set up home in every Canadian Province and played an influential role in national life. Economic interests and trading links have continued to foster mutual interest since the transfer of people has slowed down. In bringing together the material in this format it is hoped that it will become easier to explore the many facets of this Canadian-Ulster relationship and in turn add an academic dimension to the areas of mutual interest.

As the reader will quickly notice, the vast majority of the archives are deposited in the Public Record Office of Northern Ireland. The main body of artefacts are to be found in the Inuit and Indian collections of the Ulster Museum. Both of these institutions are in Belfast. This might not be unexpected for such a small area but it was slightly surprising that the other repositories in the Province did not have more substantial holdings. Searches were conducted in all of the libraries and museums and consultations took place with all the interested parties in Northern Ireland. Perhaps, as interest increases in local history, the public will be encouraged to deposit family papers with local institutions and hence bring to light those Canadian letters which, I feel, must exist but which still lie buried in attics around the country.

It is because of the preponderance of PRONI holdings that I have decided to follow the listing system of that institution as displayed in the Deputy Keeper's *Reports*. This will make it easier for those visiting PRONI to find their way around the archives. Of course it also means that material on any given subject is scattered throughout the catalogue. This is unavoidable as any attempt to adopt a more thematic approach would create as many problems as it would solve. An individual holding may include papers on a variety of topics such as emigration, political and commercial affairs. Thematic listing would lead to either artificial separation or to duplication, both resulting in confusion. The present system will mean that prudent use of the indices is essential and here again the PRONI layout has been copied with indices for Personal and Place Names and for General Subjects.

The holdings which the entries in this catalogue describe cover the period 1705-1992. They are of various sizes with some containing several thousand documents whilst others might only have a single letter or photograph. Similarly, some form what might be considered the Canadian section of a much larger holding, as is the case with many family papers. The subject variety is, of course, immense. Ulster men have played their part in the exploration of Canada either as motivators, such as Arthur Dobbs,[1] or as participants, as F.R.M. Crozier did in the Franklin expedition of 1845.[2] But obviously emigration material constitutes the main element with several hundred references. Information on the pressures at work on the Ulster people who were to make the journey is found alongside descriptions of their Canadian experience. Emigration agent records, shipping company advertisements and emigrant guides cover the topic from all angles. There is a very substantial body of emigrant correspondence, with some magnificent descriptions of their new lives. Genealogical lists document the trans-Atlantic family connections.

Other records include those of the military which highlight the role of Ulster born soldiers who fought in the British Service during the battles which shaped the political boundaries of the North American continent. The personal papers of prominent politicians and statesmen of Ulster stock, like the 1st Earl of Dufferin [3] and the 2nd Earl of Gosford,[4] who played a central role in Canadian affairs under the imperial regime, stand alongside the records of the Northern Ireland Government which sought to legitimize its position by encouraging co-operation with what it considered to be its Canadian friends. These papers are particularly important as they have received little attention hitherto. As the political and sectarian divides widened in the late nineteenth and early twentieth centuries, Ulster men of all persuasions sought support from allies in Canada and organisations such as the Orange Order and the Irish Home Rule League are represented here.

There is also a large collection of business records which indicate the extent of the economic ties. Shipping companies had as important a role to play here as they did in transporting emigrants and the records of companies like J. & J. Cooke & McCorkell [5] describe the nature of this dual role.

Whilst every holding has some intrinsic interest there are some which, although of less general import, are perhaps more colourful and interesting in their own right. Alexander Robb's collection of photographs of British Columbia in the 1860s and 1870s [6] and Ernest Cochrane's descriptions of life as a member of the Mounties in the 1880s and 1890s [7] are two such examples.

I sincerely hope that this catalogue will be of use to everyone who has an interest in the Ulster-Canadian connection, whether it be from a personal perspective or from a more general academic standpoint. The archives described are full of human experience, happy, mundane and tragic. They offer Ulster people the opportunity to see the influence their corner has had on the wider world and for Canadians the chance to discover something more of the character of the people who have had such an impact on their history.

Many people throughout the Province have been of enormous help during my search. Often their efforts were in vain as nothing was discovered, but this did not diminish their enthusiasm to co-operate. Those whom I wish to thank individually are: Trevor Parkhill of the Public Record Office of Northern Ireland; Lorraine Tennant of the Ulster-American Folk Park; Winnifred Glover of the Ulster Museum; Seamus Smyth of Maynooth College; and Charlie Gallagher of Londonderry. I would also like to thank the staff of the following:

> Public Record Office of Northern Ireland, Belfast.
> Queen's University, Belfast.
> Ulster Museum, Belfast
> Central Library, Belfast
> Ulster Folk and Transport Museum, Cultra
> Ulster-American Folk Park, Omagh
> Linenhall Library, Belfast
> Newry and Mourne Arts Centre, Newry
> Down Museum, Downpatrick
> Lisburn Museum, Lisburn
> Armagh County Museum, Armagh
> Fermanagh County Museum, Enniskillen
> The Federation for Ulster Local Studies

Belfast Education and Library Board
North Eastern Education and Library Board
South Eastern Education and Library Board
Western Education and Library Board

The text was indexed by Colin Wisdom.

1. See D.562
2. See T.1424
5. See D.2892

3. See D.1071
4. See D.2259
6. See D.3758

7. See T.3504

ILLUSTRATIONS

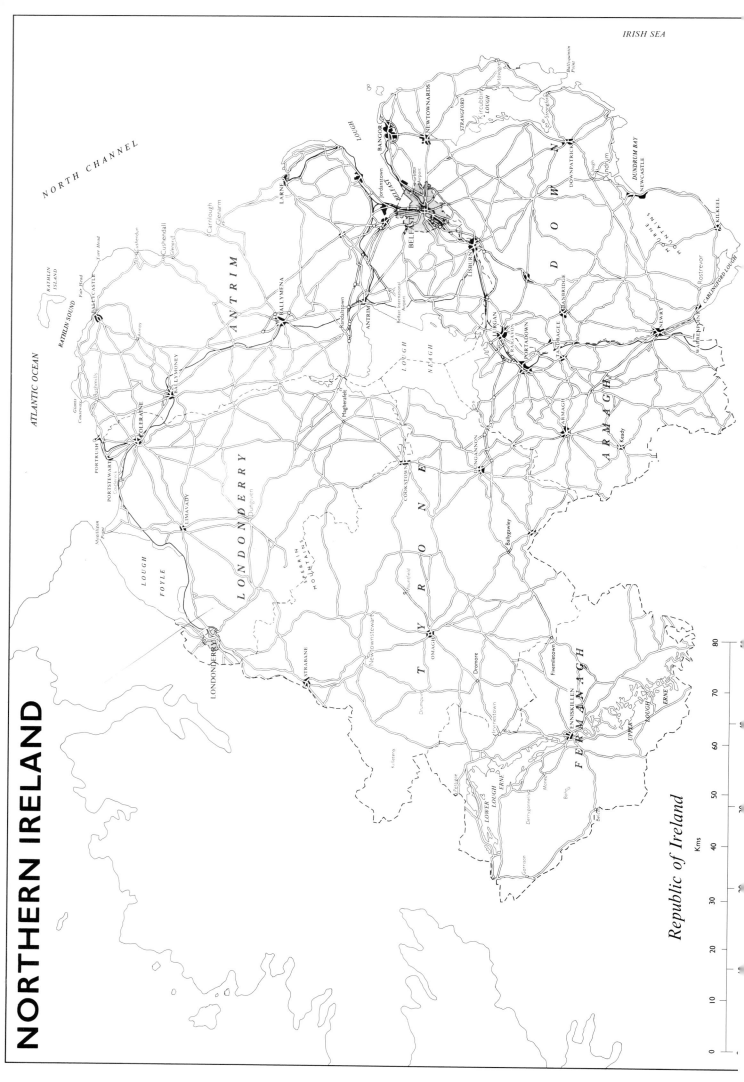

NORTHERN IRELAND

Republic of Ireland

IRISH SEA

NORTH CHANNEL

ATLANTIC OCEAN

RATHLIN ISLAND

RATHLIN SOUND

D O W N

A N T R I M

L O N D O N D E R R Y

T Y R O N E

A R M A G H

F E R M A N A G H

LOUGH NEAGH

LOUGH FOYLE

SPERRIN MOUNTAINS

MOURNE MOUNTAINS

STRANGFORD LOUGH

KILLOUGH LOUGH

DUNDRUM BAY

CARLINGFORD LOUGH

UPPER LOUGH ERNE

LOWER LOUGH ERNE

BELFAST
Belfast International Airport

LONDONDERRY

NEWRY

ARMAGH

OMAGH

ENNISKILLEN

COLERAINE

LARNE

BANGOR

NEWTOWNARDS

LISBURN

LURGAN

PORTADOWN

BANBRIDGE

DOWNPATRICK

NEWCASTLE

KILKEEL

WARRENPOINT

BALLYMENA

ANTRIM

BALLYMONEY

BALLYCASTLE

PORTRUSH

PORTSTEWART

LIMAVADY

STRABANE

COOKSTOWN

MAGHERAFELT

DUNGANNON

NEWTOWNSTEWART

RANDALSTOWN

Jordanstown

Carnlough

Glenarm

Cushendun

Cushendall

Glenariff

Fair Head

Torr Head

Bushmills

Giants Causeway

Castlerock

Dungiven

Magilligan Point

Mountfield

Dromore

Ballygawley

Fivemiletown

Drumquin

Irvinestown

Killeter

Dromore

Garrison

Derrygonnelly

Belleek

Kesh

Boho

Maguiresbridge

Keady

Tandragee

Craigavon

Portglenone

Portavogie

Ballyquintin Point

Kircubbin

Killyleagh

Ardglass

Dundrum

Rostrevor

Kms
0   10   20   30   40   50   60   70   80

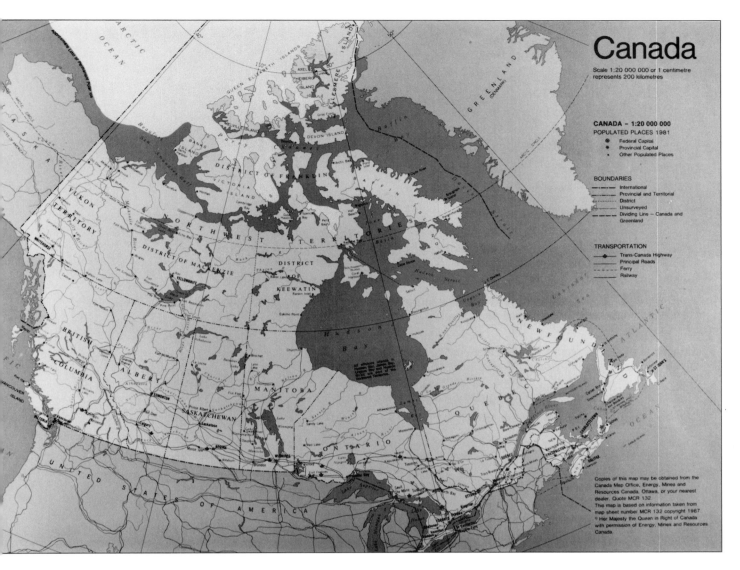

Reproduced from *Canada: a portrait*, Catalogue no. CS11-403E, Minister of Supply and Services, Canada, 1992, p.201; with the permission of the Minister of Industry, Science and Technology, Canada, 1993.

This map provided through the co-operation of Statistics Canada. Readers wishing further information may obtain copies of related publications by mail from Publications' Sales, Statistics Canada, Ottawa, K1A, OT6, by telephone 1-613-951-7277 national toll-free 1-800-267-6677. You may also facsimile your order by dialling 1-613-951-1584.

1. **PUBLIC RECORD OFFICE OF NORTHERN IRELAND**

By far the largest collection of Canadian material in Northern Ireland can be found in the Public Record Office in Balmoral Avenue, Belfast. This collection can be subdivided under various headings relating to the place of origin. The first distinct group are the records of the Northern Ireland Government, which can again be subdivided under the various Departments to which they pertain. Other official sources include the Boards of Guardians' records, the Harbour Commissioners' records and the papers of the Ministry of Transport, London. The second subdivision consists of the Church records and these relate to the Roman Catholic Church and to the various Protestant denominations. The third and largest group of holdings are the private records. These can be further subdivided under the headings of 'D.' original documents and 'T.' transcripts. These records form the major part of this catalogue. Finally, those holdings which are on microfilm are listed under 'MIC.'. Although these include copies of documents held in PRONI, only those microfilms which are not duplicated elsewhere are listed here.

PRONI holdings cover a vast range of topics and personalities. The Northern Ireland Government records illustrate the links which existed between Stormont and Ottawa and the interest the Unionist Government had in fostering the Canadian connection. They are particularly important as they have been largely neglected hitherto. The private records are the most disparate, ranging from the papers of prominent men in the public sphere to semi-literate letters from impoverished emigrants. There is a vast body of emigration material alongside commercial records, shipping lists, genealogies, school records, biographical and autobiographical sketches, travelogues, regimental records, advertisements, printed works, newspapers, photographs, paintings and maps. There are some 690 entries in the PRONI section of this list but it should also be remembered that whilst each separate holding is regarded as one entry, some entries may include a large number of documents. This is best illustrated by the example of P.M.6/12/3 which is the file relating to Sir James Craig's visit to Canada in 1926. Although it constitutes only one entry, the file actually contains several hundred letters, memoranda and related papers.

<u>RECORDS OF GOVERNMENT DEPARTMENTS</u>

UNITED KINGDOM

MINISTRY OF TRANSPORT

c.100,000 documents. They include ships' agreements, crew lists and official log books of merchant vessels registered or built in Ireland, 1862-1938. The information they contain includes details of the vessels' names, port of registration, port of departure and destination, and details of the owners and masters. The crew lists cover names, ages, places of birth, home addresses, next of kin, previous ship, and date and cause of leaving. Although this holding does not include all returns of Northern Ireland interest, since some were retained by the Public Record Office, London, and the National Maritime Museum, it does contain a great deal of information about shipping between Canada and Ulster.
TRANS. 2A

NORTHERN IRELAND

MINISTRY OF AGRICULTURE

Fisheries

File, 1928-53, concerning the proposed importation of salmon ova from Canada by the Foyle and Bann Fisheries Company. One of the Company's directors, A.H. Noble, travelled to Ottawa to negotiate a deal and sought the assistance of the Northern Ireland Government in gaining the co-operation of the Canadian Fisheries Department. F.W. Field, H.M. Senior Trade Commissioner in Montreal, Quebec, was asked to act as an intermediary. The Foyle and Bann Fisheries Company's Head Office in Liverpool is noted as being a major handler of Canadian frozen fish and poultry exported to the United Kingdom.
AG.6/1/57

Policy

File, 1932, containing a memorandum by J.M. Andrews, the Minister of Labour, on the policy to be adopted by the Northern Ireland delegation at the Imperial Economic Conference at Ottawa in 1932.
AG.16/11/2

CABINET SECRETARIAT

Note: Cabinet Secretariat files were organised to deal with the several responsibilities of the various Ministries.

Finance

Files, 1926-53, concerning Northern Ireland Government entertainment expenditure on official visits of various Canadian individuals and parties. These included W. Munroe, P.M. of Newfoundland, (1926), G. H. Ferguson, P.M. of Ontario, (1930), and R.B. Bennett, P.M. of Canada, (1930).
CAB.9A/7/7, 13, 16, 26, 31, 34, 45, 72, 84

File, 1931-2, on the Northern Ireland budget, with references to the effects of decisions taken at the Imperial Economic Conference at Ottawa in 1932.
CAB.9A/14/3

Labour

File, 1928, concerning Northern Ireland's allocation of places in the U.K. total of 10,000 for the Canadian Harvesters' Scheme, an Empire Migration scheme. Initially Northern Ireland was overlooked but, after protests, a quota was allocated which the Ministry of Labour regarded as too small and negotiations began to have the number increased to 250. These were unsuccessful.
CAB.9C/29

Agriculture

File, 1931-58, concerning the implications for Northern Ireland of the Diseases of Animals Regulations in force in Canada.
CAB.9E/3/22

File, 1931-6, concerning the implications for Northern Ireland of the Destructive Insects and Pests Regulations in force in Canada.
CAB.9E/7/2

File, 1923-7, on the development of agriculture in Northern Ireland, including references to the loss through emigration of innovative and adaptive Ulstermen to Canada.
CAB.9E/23/1

File, 1922-30, concerning the exportation of potatoes to the United States, Canada and New-foundland.
CAB.9E/50/1

File, 1923-34, concerning Canada's recognition of the standards of Northern Ireland's Seed Testing Station.
CAB.9E/121/1

File, 1934-7, concerning Northern Ireland's involvement in the Canadian proposed Common-wealth Scientific Conference. The file contains a letter from Stanley Baldwin, Prime Minister of Great Britain, to Sir John Gilmour, outlining Canada's role.
CAB.9E/124/1

Commerce

File, 1923-55, concerning the tariffs levied by various countries, including Canada, on imported goods.
CAB.9F/2/1-2

File, 1928-30, with reference to Canadian perceptions of Northern Ireland. In 1928 there was concern about the presence of inferior linen products on the Canadian markets which were being passed off as originating in Northern Ireland. In 1930 information indicating favourable trends in the Northern Ireland economy was supplied to the Rev. K. Hunter Palmer, Westminster Presbyterian Church, Hamilton, Ontario, to enable him to refute criticisms of Northern Ireland made by Senator George Lynch Stanton in the *Hamilton Herald* following a visit to Northern Ireland.
CAB.9F/7/1

File, 1933, concerning flax growing within Northern Ireland and throughout the Empire, with references to Canadian production.
CAB.9F/8/1

File, 1924, concerning the exportation of roses to Canada.
CAB.9F/20/1

Files, 1932-7, concerning Northern Ireland's involvement in the Imperial Economic Conferences in Ottawa, (1932), and in London, (1937). They contain material referring to all aspects of the organisation including the appointment of representatives, agenda, travel arrangements, social functions, channels of communication and reports on the work which was completed. There is also reference to the establishment of a committee on Economic Consultation and Co-operation and its dealing with matters arising from the Ottawa conference.
CAB.9F/57/1-2

File, 1933, containing miscellaneous correspondence concerning the Empire Marketing Board. This includes a reference to a visit of the Director of the British Standards Association of Canada, Australia and New Zealand to Northern Ireland.
CAB.9F/58/1

File, 1929-57, concerning the fostering of commercial links between Canada and Northern Ireland. This included the appointment of a Canadian Trade Commissioner in 1931 and details are given of the arrangements made to facilitate his work. Statistics referring to Ulster-Canadian trade between 1953-5 are also included.
CAB.9F/107/1

File, 1930, concerning inter-Empire trade and containing proposals for regular conferences with the Dominions to foster such commerce.
CAB.9F/117/1

File, 1930, concerning the entry of Scotch and Irish whiskies to Quebec.
CAB.9F/119/1

File, 1950, concerning the visit of the Northern Ireland Prime Minister, Sir Basil Brooke to the United States and Canada. It is closed to the public for 50 years.
CAB.9F/123/26

File, 1944-56, sub-headed 'Government Propaganda and Publicity'. It deals with the Northern Ireland Government's subsidization of the book *Ulster Sails West* by Rev. W.F. Marshall which was regarded as a foil to the opposition to the Northern Ireland regime in Canada and the United States.
CAB.9F/123/28

File, 1947, sub-headed 'Government Propaganda and Publicity' and entitled 'Publicity in America'. It includes copies of the minutes of the meetings of the Cabinet Publicity Committee which discussed efforts to engage a *Toronto Sentinel* reporter called Armstrong to provide the Ulster Office with news items which appeared in the Canadian Press and which were detrimental to Northern Ireland interests. This was intended to enable the Ulster Office in London to issue an immediate reply. There is also a small body of correspondence between Northern Ireland Government officials, including the Northern Ireland Prime Minister Sir Basil Brooke, and Governor Alexander, Government House, Ottawa, in which Alexander speaks of his personal friendship with Brooke and offers his assistance to Ulstermen who were visiting Canada on

behalf of the Northern Ireland Administration. Such visitors also referred to in the file were J.G. Bridges, Director General of the Travel Association, W. Douglas of the Unionist Party and General Brooke Purdon, the Ulster Agent in London.
CAB.9F/123/107

Files, 1951-6, sub-headed 'Government Propaganda and Publicity' and concerning Northern Ireland Government publicity in North Amercia. Closed to the public until 2002.
CAB.9F/123/111-112

File, 1933-5, concerning the opening of a shop to sell Canadian produce in Belfast.
CAB.9F/142

File, 1944, concerning the creation of a transatlantic air service. The Stormont Government sought to establish air bases for such flights in Northern Ireland. The file contains information on pre- and post war transport links with Canada and refers to the attendance of S.O. Hicks, the Northern Ireland representative, at the 1944 Civil Aviation Conference in Montreal, Quebec. Also included is a printed booklet produced by R.A.F. Transport Command entitled *Report on a Tour of Routes, 1944*. It documents the investigations of E.C. Bowyer, the Chief of the Information Department, and includes references to a visit to Canada where he discussed transatlantic air links with various interested bodies. Amongst these were officials of the Canadian Ministry of Transport and representatives of Trans-Canada Airlines, Canadian-Vickers and the Canadian Power Boat Company.
CAB.9F/151/2

File, 1946, including correspondence concerning the establishment of a subsidiary of Yorkshire Knitting Mills of Toronto, Ontario, in Northern Ireland. Representatives of the Company visited Ulster on a fact-finding mission in 1946.
CAB.9F/163

File, 1943, concerning the Northern Ireland Government's desire to have the province included in a B.B.C. Radio programme called *Transatlantic Call* which highlighted links between Canada and Great Britain but excluded Northern Ireland.
CAB.9F/165/3

Files, 1949-56, concerning the establishment of factories in Northern Ireland by American and Canadian industrialists. Also included is material referring to the visit of Col. S.G. Haughton to the United States and Canada to investigate the possibility of developing greater trading links between both countries and Northern Ireland. A copy of his report is inserted.
CAB.9F/187/1-2

File, 1958, concerning the visit to Canada and the United States of the Lord Mayor of Belfast, Major W.C. McKee. It includes details of the organisation of the trip with a copy of the itinerary.
CAB.9F/198

Law and Justice

File, 1929-30, concerning the selection of suitable lawyers in the United States to act on behalf of British subjects with interests in North America.
CAB.9I/20

Miscellaneous

File on International Congresses, 1927-52, concerning Northern Ireland's representation. Amongst these are several which took place in Canada.
CAB.9IC/8

Imperial Government correspondence, 1932, containing miscellaneous references to Northern Ireland's involvement in the Imperial Economic Conference at Ottawa in 1932.
CAB.9R/57/6

MINISTRY OF COMMERCE

Tourist Development Committee

Letter and memorandum, 3 October 1938, concerning the establishment, functions and activities of the Canadian Travel Bureau.
COM.11/2/10/10

GPO liaison

File, 1929, concerning the Transatlantic Telephone Service, including a European-America Telephone Service list of the principal towns in Canada to which the service was available and the charges made.
COM.21/24

File, 1931, concerning fines imposed upon postal packets from Canada to Northern Ireland because of incorrect marking of contents.
COM.21/27

U.K.-U.S.A., Trade Negotiations

File, 1937-38, concerning the U.K.-U.S.A. trade negotiations of 1938 which included Newfoundland in their remit. Some of the papers are closed until 2014.
COM.22

Establishment

Files, 1941-4, containing permits for business journeys abroad, including some to Canada.
COM.23/437-438

Flax Seed Committee

File, 1926, including an excerpt from the *Mercantile Trust Review of the Pacific* which refers to flax fibre production in Canada.
COM.25/2

Trade Statistics

Files, 1922-32, recording export/imports for the port of Belfast. From 1922-6 only exports are covered and the entries are weekly. For 1932 there are monthly returns for both exports and imports. Some details are given of the commodities involved and Canadian ports are among those dealt with.
COM.38/3/1-3

Commerce and Economics

File, 1922, concerning the possibility of Harry Ferguson establishing a factory to manufacture his ploughs in Canada.
COM.62/1/11

File, 1921-35, concerning Board of Trade certification of Meat Force products intended for exportation to Canada.
COM.62/1/121

Files, 1927-53, concerning the Northern Ireland linen industry's export market in Canada. These include a series of complaints about Canadian treatment of Ulster products, usually directed at duty impositions. There are also details of the industry's organisation of opposition, with Stormont assistance, to proposed increases in Canadian tariff duties on linen imports. In 1934 the textiles adviser to the Canadian Department of National Revenue, A.C. Williams, visited Northern Ireland to discuss linen duties and there are references to the negotiations and copies of the agreement reached. Some files also contain copies of publications which refer to the Canadian linen market, with accompanying official memoranda on the Northern Ireland industry's position in it.
COM.61/1/133, 236, 327, 391, 410, 420, 572, 681, 684, 917 and COM.75/3/7-8

File, 1927-39, concerning a request from the Canadian Department of Agriculture's Experimental farm at Ottawa for details of the Watson-Waddell flax retting process. A sample of the flax straw is included in the file.
COM.62/1/142

File, 1926-8, concerning the supply of Irish linen to newly-erected, first class hotels in Canada. Information about these hotels was passed to the Stormont Government by the Canadian Trade Commissioner for Scotland and Northern Ireland, G.B. Johnson.
COM.62/1/159/1

File, 1932, concerning the arrangements for the Northern Ireland delegation's attendance at the Imperial Economic Conference at Ottawa.
COM.62/1/271

Files, 1932-5, containing representations made to the Northern Ireland Government by various industries, complaining of difficulties they experienced in exporting to Canada. Prior to the 1932 Imperial Economic Conference, the Stormont Administration asked for details of problems which the industries of the province met with in dealing with other areas of the Empire. The complaints usually centre on the restrictive nature of Canadian tariffs but there is also an accusation of 'dumping' by the Canadian milling industry. Other industries which submitted representations were soapmakers, mineral water producers, clothmakers, the woollen industry, linen thread producers, the tobacco industry and agriculture. In some cases there is a follow up correspondence after the conference.
COM.62/1/294-300, 385

File, 1933-5, concerning the establishment of a shop in Arthur Street, Belfast, to sell Canadian produce in Northern Ireland. The file includes many newspaper cuttings describing the shop's opening.
COM.62/1/383

File, 1932-6, concerning an accusation by Ross Bros Ltd, Belfast, that their exports to Canada were hampered by the imposition of unfair duties. The Northern Ireland Government investi-

gated this complaint and enquired whether or not goods from the South of Ireland entered Canada on the same terms as those from the Northern jurisdiction.
COM.62/1/391/3

File, 1934, concerning the proposal by F.R. Phelan, President of Financial Service Ltd, Montreal, Quebec, to include in the firm's Press service, information on those Northern Ireland companies which had business interests in Canada.
COM.62/1/400

File, 1935, concerning the efforts of the Department of Overseas Trade to stimulate trade with Canada. Various Northern Ireland companies requested information and assistance following the distribution of a circular letter on the subject by the Northern Ireland Government.
COM.62/1/451

File, 1936, concerning the Canadian Department of National Revenue's indication of the tariff status of imported towels.
COM.62/1/572/1

File, 1938, concerning the request of T.M. Kirkwood, Toronto, Ontario, for a contract to import Irish peat into Canada.
COM.62/1/671

File, 1938, concerning the complaint of Dunvilles Ltd, Belfast, against a new regulation issued by the Quebec Liquor Commission on the blending of Irish and Scotch whiskies.
COM.62/1/688

File, 1938, concerning the Tourist Development Committee's investigation of other countries policies on tourism, and includes an examination of the Canadian Travel Bureau's activities. There is some correspondence with the Chief of the C.T.B., Leo Dolan.
COM.62/1/738

File, 1950-56, concerning Sir Basil Brooke's tour of the United States and Canada in 1950.
COM.61/1/1193

Printed Trade Statistics

Printed ledger, 1924, of Northern Ireland trade statistics, with details of imports and exports with Canada for that year. The quantities and values for individual commodities are also given.
COM.75/4/2

File, 1936, concerning Northern Ireland's sea borne trade, with details of trade with Canada in that year.
COM.75/11/1

MINISTRY OF FINANCE

Files, 1926-41, concerning the establishment and administration of the Richhill Training Centre for emigrants. The Co. Armagh centre was opened to give assistance to those unemployed young men who had been prohibited from taking advantage of the assisted passage schemes under the Empire Settlement Act (1922) because of their lack of agricultural experience. Reference is made to the numbers who were helped by their Richhill training to get to Canada and details are given of the kind of help they received, including passage funding. Indications are provided about the areas in which the emigrants settled. The centre was closed in 1941.
FIN.18/6/39 and **FIN.18/7/55**

File, 1928-9, concerning the supply of Ulstermen to assist with the Canadian harvest. Northern Ireland was given a quota of 100 men out of a total of 10,000 required by the Dominion. Information is given on travel arrangements, payment, medical attention, loans and pre-journey training. It was hoped that many of those who went would stay in Canada.
FIN.18/7/35

File, 1936-8, concerning the Northern Ireland Government's investigation of the feasibility of underwriting the credit facilities of Harland & Wolff's Belfast shipyard should the shipyard be given an order for two liners from the Canadian Pacific Railway Company. This involved a close examination of the financial position of the C.P.R. and the material includes maps of the Company's areas of operation and a list of all the shipping stock it owned. In the end the whole venture was abandoned.
FIN.18/16/255

Files, 1932-3, containing preparatory papers and policy documents for the Northern Ireland delegation which attended the 1932 Imperial Economic Conference at Ottawa. There are also follow-up papers indicating the effects on Northern Ireland of the Conference's recommendations.
FIN.30/AA/96 and **FIN.30/AC/2**

File, 1949, containing a report on the Commonwealth Conference held at Bigwin, Ontario, by Lt Col Connolly Gage. The file is closed to the public for 75 years.
FIN.30/AB/27

File, 1948, concerning the Canadian visit of Major Maynard Sinclair, Minister for Finance. It includes details of the arrangements for the trip and his itinerary, with copies of letters from the directors of James Mackie & Sons, Belfast, to Canadian contacts asking that they show Major Sinclair hospitality and assistance on his visit.
FIN.30/FC/66

Diary, 10 July-23 August 1932, kept by H.M. Pollock, Minister of Finance, during his attendance at the Imperial Economic Conference at Ottawa. Pollock describes the journey to Canada of the Northern Ireland delegation, including the negotiations held on board ship with Imperial Government officials. Of particular concern were the effects of the high Canadian tariffs on the Ulster linen industry. His record of the events on arrival at Ottawa covers both the formal and informal gatherings and is punctuated with personal comments and observations. He provides a detailed description of the opening ceremony and refers to various business meetings held with other delegations. Pollock and his colleagues sought to forward the Unionist cause at Ottawa and he felt that some useful contacts had been established. Before returning home they were able to make a short tour, including trips to Niagara Falls, Quebec and Montreal.
FIN.30/L/2

File, 1925, concerning the visit to Northern Ireland of Peter Larkin, the Canadian High Commissioner in London, and the preparations made by Sir James Craig, Prime Minister of Northern Ireland, to entertain him. A photograph, taken from the *Toronto Saturday Night*, shows Larkin and his wife with Craig and Lord and Lady Londonderry at Mount Stewart, Co. Down. There is also a letter to Craig from F. Daul, Imperial Grand Orange Council of the World, Toronto, Ontario, giving notice that G.H. Ferguson, P.M. of Ontario, was to visit Ireland. Daul refers to him as '.... One of our own sort in every way .....'.
PM.6/1

File, 1926-40, concerning the visit to Canada of Sir James Craig, in 1926 and subsequent correspondence on Canadian matters, most of it arising from the visit. He was invited by Peter Larkin

and the file contains full details of the organisation of the trip and of his itinerary, which included visits to Montreal, Ottawa, Winnipeg, Edmonton, Jasper, Prince Rupert, Vancouver, Victoria, Saskatoon, Toronto, Niagara and Quebec, between 18 August and 2 October. Craig received a large body of correspondence from a wide variety of disparate sources, including many letters from the Canadian Orange Lodges. References are also included as to the assessment of the trip by Canadians and there are numerous newspaper cuttings from Canadian papers.
PM.6/12/3

File, 1930-43, concerning Northern Ireland's participation in the Overseas League, including the attendance of Canadian speakers at the Ulster Group's meetings and the organisation of a League tour for 200 people to eastern Canada in 1937.
PM.6/64

File, 1951-7, containing the correspondence between Sir Robert Gransden, the Cabinet Secretary, and Lt Col Baptist Johnston, Honorary President of the Canadian-based Irish Protestant Benevolent Society. Most of the correspondence is of a personal nature, with both men using their friendship to have friends and associates introduced to the highest echelons when they crossed the Atlantic in either direction. On some occasions there is a more formal exchange of advice or information.
PM.8/48

Files, 1950, concerning the visit of Sir Basil Brooke, Prime Minister of Northern Ireland, to Canada with details of the organisation and itinerary which took him from Ottawa to Toronto and then on to Montreal and Quebec between 9-25 May. The copies of the notes on those whom Brooke was to meet contain details of religion.
PM.11/7, 8

Unsorted general correspondence, 1939-70, of the Ulster Tourist Development Association. Concerned with increasing the number of foreign visitors to Northern Ireland, the Association had many correspondents including some in Canada. There were enquiries from individual Canadians who wished to visit the Province and communications with Canadian firms and agencies, such as Trans-Canada Airlines, the Canadian Pacific Railway Co., T. Eaton and Co., and *Canadian Weekly* magazine, which had an interest in tourism in Northern Ireland.
TOUR.1/3/7-9, 25, 27

RECORDS OF PUBLIC BODIES

BOARDS OF GUARDIANS' RECORDS

These consist of the records of nearly 30 Poor Law Unions which served the whole of Ulster from 1839 to 1922 and in some areas are continued up to 1948. The principal sources of Canadian interest are the minute books of the Boards for the period to 1870 and particularly 1844-55. The records of Unions such as Newtownlimavady, Londonderry, Strabane, Coleraine and particularly Ballymoney relate assisted emigrations to Canada of families of pauper inmates, particularly female orphans. Often there are lists of names of individuals nominated for emigration and there are also practical details of the arrangements for their voyages. PRONI also holds records of some of the Unions which are in the jurisdiction of the Republic of Ireland.
BG.1-29 and BG.42, 43, 59, 65, 69, 83, 87, 98, 108, 115, 116, 118, 145, 163

PRIVATELY DEPOSITED RECORDS

Letters, petitions, notebooks, diaries, pamphlets and other documents, 1727-64, principally of Arthur Dobbs of Carrickfergus, Co. Antrim. Dobbs held estates in the American colonies and

was Governor of North Carolina, 1754-65. He was particularly interested in increasing commerce between Britain and Ireland and North America and he corresponded on this subject with senior figures in the British administration, including Sir Robert Walpole and the 1st Earl Granville. His letters focus on the role of the Hudson's Bay Company: Dobbs collected papers which described the various expeditions seeking a North-West Passage, an enterprise in which he was keenly interested, and other expeditions concerned with land exploration in Canada. The journal of Henry Kelsey (transcribed and annotated in *The Kelsey Papers*) is the most important item in the latter category. In addition, there are two manuscript notebooks related to the Quebec campaign of the Seven Years' War and a number of letters concerned with Dobbs' dispensation of his patronage in Canada. The portions relating to Canada have been copied by the National Archives of Canada as MG.18 D4.
D.162

Letter book, 1873-8, of the Home Rule League of Ireland. It includes many letters to supporters and sympathisers in Canada. These document the establishment of similar associations in Canada and illustrate the fund-raising activities and public tours carried on there in the League's name.
D.213 pp 62-63, 74-78, 91-92, 99-102, 126-127, 130-134, 138-139, 155-156, 158-159, 176-177, 183-206, 244-245

Anonymous journal, October-December 1833, of a voyage on board the ship *Glasgow* from Liverpool, England, to New York. There are references to other passengers bound for Canada and passing references to Newfoundland. Other ships encountered *en route* included the *Pomona*, sailing from Quebec to Liverpool.
D.280

Two volumes, 1852-65, of the visitors' book to the Imperial Hotel, Belfast. It includes the names of many Canadians.
D.284

Letter book, 1704-07, of a Belfast merchant, [Isaac McCartney?]. The letters contain details of his business ventures, including trading voyages to North America, with references to the transportation of barrelled beef to Newfoundland. There is also a letter dated, 26 March 1705, from Alexander and Henry Cairnes [?], concerning an insurance claim on the ship *Lawrell* which had been damaged whilst lying for seven months at Newfoundland.
D.501

Letter, 28 July 1840, and photograph album, 1881-4, of Major (later General) Andrew Nugent. The letter was written from Fredericton, New Brunswick, to his brother at Portaferry, Co. Down, and describes life in the army in Canada. He also comments on the new steamers which have just started to cross the Atlantic and a visit of the Governor General to Halifax, Nova Scotia. The photograph album contains many Canadian views.
D.552/A/9/6/3 and **/B/3/5/2-3**

Letters, copy letters, reports and memorials, 1765-1821, of John Foster, 1st Baron Oriel, (1740-1828), and of his father, Anthony Foster. John Foster was Chief Baron of the Exchequer, 1766-77, and both father and son were closely associated with the Linen Board. The main series of letters are between John Foster and various correspondents concerning the possible importation of flaxseed from Canada and the payment of bounties for it. Other papers include a memorial of William Todd, late of Canada, to the Linen Board asking for financial assistance for his bleach green and a letter concerning the seizure of a vessel at St John's, Newfoundland. In addition there are three reports relating to commerce between Britain and Ireland on the one hand and North America on the other. Two of these concern the quantity of linen exported from Ireland to

North America in the decades 1794-1804 and 1798-1808. The other report presents a wider view of trade in this direction between Christmas 1765 and Christmas 1766 and focusses upon the individual British plantations, including Hudson's Bay.
D.562/1480, 1818, 5984, 5993-6007, 6073, 6075, 6837

Four letters, 16 February 1791-May 1804, of Sir George Macartney, Lissanoure, Co. Antrim, 1st Earl Macartney (1737-1806), one of the foremost British ambassadors of his day. The earliest letter is from Sir John Johnston, Governor of Upper Canada, commenting upon his qualifications and his influence with the Indians and soliciting Macartney's influence to secure for him the post of manager of the Jesuits' property which, he felt, might be developed to support a university instead of a poor seminary. The other letters concern Sir E. Gower Horndean's attempts to be appointed commander of the Newfoundland naval station and Macartney's role in that enterprise. Copies of letters to Viscount Melville are included.
D.572/8/35, 199 and **/15/3**

61 letters, 17 March 1833-1851, concerning Thomas Greeves's role as the attorney of the late James Heather, Drumharrif, Dungannon, Co. Tyrone. The first five letters refer to Greeves's appointment as the attorney of James Heather of Montreal, son of the deceased. The rest of the correspondence concerns the settlement of the disputed will and the correspondents include: James Heather, Montreal and New York; William Heather, Brockville, Upper Canada; J McClellan, Montreal; Anna Heather, Brockville, Upper Canada; Welford and Elizabeth Heather, Kildare, Upper Canada; Mary Heather Junior, Kildare, Upper Canada; and Mr Knox, Montreal.

Also, pedigree, compiled in 1951, of the Heather family and dating their origins from 1746.
D.593/2-6, 7-62

Letter, 21 June 1779, from Robert Hodgson, 8 Mount Row, [London], to Lord Hillsborough, Secretary of State for the American Colonies, [London], with a general plan of operation for the West Indies as a naval base for the containment of the 13 American colonies. There are passing references to the naval bases in Canada.
D.607/B/99A

Journal, 1817-21, of A.C. Dawson written during his service on board *H.M.S. Tigris, H.M.S. Spartan, H.M.S. Pyramid* and *H.M.S. Niemen*. There are passing references to Halifax, Nova Scotia, on two pages.
D.618/36B, p. 86 and **p. 186**

Letter, 1931, from Baron Stamfordham, King George V's private secretary, [London], to the 3rd Duke of Abercorn, Barons Court, Co. Tyrone, expressing the King's regret that the Duke had declined the offer of the Governorship General of Canada.
D.623/A/354

Correspondence and typescript notes, 1926, of Robert Montgomery, Vancouver, British Columbia, concerning his work on the genealogy of the Montgomery family of Ireland and Canada.
D.627/451-452

Legal papers, 20 September 1872-22 October 1889, concerning the following individuals: Richard Purdon, Toronto, Ontario; Henry Purdon Bell, Winnipeg, Manitoba; and William Carter, Toronto, Ontario.
D.639/271, 283b, 330, 340

List, 1890-1921, of members of the Girls' Friendly Society who emigrated from Counties Armagh, Tyrone, Londonderry, Louth and Donegal. It provides the names of the girls involved,

date of departure, ship's name, home address, destination and subsequent address, their associate's address and a section entitled 'Introduction to colony and remarks'. The Canadian destinations included: Toronto, Trenton, Kingston, Niagara and Hamilton in Ontario; Victoria and Vancouver in British Columbia; Calgary, Alberta; and Montreal, Quebec.
D.648/9

Three letters, 6 May 1863-15 June 1869, received by George Dunbar, [Ireland]. The first two, from Alexander Irwin, Armagh, and Elizabeth Eden, Eaton Square, London, refer to the emigration to Canada of a James Jones and the effect this has on his family. The third letter, from Mrs T.C. Sheppard, Quebec, concerns Dunbar's inheritance of the Canadian lands of John McQuarters who died in 1814.
D.664/D/227, 228A and 351

Unlisted letters, 1810-45, from John Murray, land agent of the Blessington estate, Co. Wicklow, and various other Irish correspondents, to the 3rd Marquess of Downshire, concerning the management of Blessington. They include references to the emigration of tenants to North America. Reference is also made to contact with Sir Jeffery Amherst, 1st Lord Amherst in Canada and to the military service of members of the Hill family in Canada.
D.671/C/214/1-483 and /C/230/1-83

Diary, 17 July-9 September 1760, covering the Quebec campaign and the events leading to the fall of Montreal to the British. The author of the diary is unknown but he was probably an officer on the staff of General Murray and, as he appears to have had an intimate knowledge of all that occurred, he may have been a secretary. This is strengthened by the inclusion in the diary of copies of correspondence, July-August 1759, which passed between Generals Wolfe and Murray. These include Wolfe's order giving alternative plans for the capture of Quebec and asking for comments, and the minutes of the Council of War between the Generals in compliance with the order. They also include information on the state of the troops in Canada, their numbers and deployment, and descriptions of the French emplacements.
D.678

New York Pocket Almanac, 1759, containing miscellaneous information on the Canadian colonies, including population estimates, roads from New York to Montreal, Quebec, distances between various points, and other miscellaneous information.
D.679

Letter, 28 October 1832, from William Campbell, surgeon, c/o James Ferguson, Peterborough, Upper Canada, to Rev. Robert Campbell, Templepatrick, Co. Antrim, describing his recent voyage to Canada and comparing his new home with his old.
D.693/7/1

Letter, 19 December 1886, from Mina C., Prince Albert, Saskatchewan, to Lily [Moore?], Craigarogan, Co. Antrim, concerning family news.
D.693/7/2

Correspondence and papers, 1871-8, of Sir Francis Hincks, Liberal Prime Minister of United Canada, 1851-4, and Minister of Finance of the Dominion, 1869-73. The papers covering the period 1871-4 concern the settlement of the estate of the Rev. Professor William Hincks. There are also four letters, 17 May-22 November 1878, from Sir Francis Hincks, Montreal, Quebec, to his cousin, Dr J.S. Drennan, Belfast, referring to Orange-Catholic rivalries in Montreal and discussing Canada's relationship with Britain and the United States.
D.729/8, 9, 18, 18A, 38-41

Extensive correspondence, accounts, order books etc., 1883-1954, of John Gunning & Co., linen manufacturers, Cookstown, Co. Tyrone. These papers include: 'colonial' daybooks nos 9-11, 1925-46, with details of sales in Canada and elsewhere; account of stock, 1911-39, held at Montreal, Quebec, and elsewhere; delivery book, 1896-7, including Montreal; confidential reports, 1907-36, prepared by R.G. Dunn & Co., Glasgow, Scotland, commenting upon the credit-worthiness of various firms, including some in Montreal and Toronto, Ontario.
D.780/6/1-4 and **/22/3, 6, 10**

Foreign order book, 1891-2, of A. & S. Henry & Co., linen manufacturers, Belfast, including sales to firms in Montreal, Quebec.
D.824

Letter, c.1849, from William Sharman Crawford, Crawfordsburn, Co. Down, to the *Dublin Evening Post*, referring to newspaper articles discussing the ill-effects of emigration.
D.856/D/96

Ten letters, 18 November 1849-10 July 1850, from various correspondents including Sir James Graham, C.S. Lefevre, Robert Peel and Lord John Russell, to William Sharman Crawford, Crawfordsburn, Co. Down, concerning his anti-emigration pamphlet entitled *Depopulation Not Necessary*.
D.856/D/97-99, 102-107, 109

Certificate, 2 July 1836, awarded to John S. Crawford on his visit to Niagara Falls.
D.856/F/47

Diaries, c.1860-1890, of William Johnston of Ballykilbeg, Lisburn, Co. Antrim. Johnston was a leading figure in the Orange Order in Ireland and he created strong contacts with Orange associations throughout Canada through visits and correspondence. These diaries document much of that contact.
D.880

Copy letter, 20 September 1843, from Edward Hanlon, Milwaukee, Wisconsin, to his father, Downpatrick, Co. Down, commenting on his experiences whilst working in Canada. He went there to look for his half brother and set up a tailoring business in the Grand River area. He was forced to move on because of an outbreak of fever and he spent five months in New London before returning to the United States. He complains of the lack of Catholic clergy in Canada.
D.885/1

Letter, 28 July 1913, from Mary Behan, U.S.A., to [?], [Ballymoate, Downpatrick, Co. Down?], commenting on a recent trip to Canada and stating that she prefers the United States.
D.885/35

Four letters, 5 July 1758-23 July 1760, from Mrs Cathcart, Chichester, England, to W. Perceval, Dublin, with news of her husband, William, and her brother, Joshua, who appear to be serving with the British forces in Canada at this time.
D.906/112, 113, 113A. 115

Printed poem, 1875, written on arrival of the ship *R B Chapman* at New Brunswick by J.S. McC.
D.913/1

Two registers, 1866-1945, of shipping vessels entering Carlingford Lough for refuge or in ballast which were liable for anchorage and harbour dues. They include references to Canadian shipping.
D.933/32-33

Legal papers, 13 September 1888, involving William S. Dunlop and his wife, Mountpleasant, Ontario, and their interest in land bought by the Giant's Causeway, Portrush and Bush Valley Railway and Tramway Co., in Co. Antrim.
D.945/10

Letter, 30 March 1799, from William Wylly, New Providence, Bahamas, to his aunt in Ireland informing her that he has been appointed King's Counsel in Nova Scotia. He also comments that two of his children are still at school in Nova Scotia.
D.955

Seven letters, 20 October 1920-21 July 1921, from George W. Knox, Victoria, British Columbia, to John Anderson, Ballynahinch, Co. Down, relating to Knox's property in Drumboneth, Co. Down.
D.961/21

Papers of the Irish Unionist Alliance, 1902-12, concerning their connections with Canada. Amongst the papers are accounts of Canadian Pacific Railway Co., stocks which the organisation sold, and a collection of unlisted papers which include details of the visit to Canada of William Lyon, M.P., in 1911-12.
D.989

Papers, 1872-9, of Frederick Temple Blackwood, 1st Earl of Dufferin, (1826-1902), during his tenure as Governor General of Canada. This is probably the most important and extensive Northern Irish holding relating to Canada. The papers are subdivided here in the same order as they are found in the comprehensive PRONI list and are as follows:

Correspondence, 21 March 1872-9 November 1878, between Lord Dufferin and the Canadian Prime Ministers, Sir John MacDonald and Alexander MacKenzie concerning official business; Correspondence, 27 March 1872-16 January 1879, between Lord Dufferin and Canadian national and provincial leaders. The subjects discussed include: Lord Dufferin's appointment and departure, imperial, legislative and administrative matters concerning the Governor General's Office; legal and constitutional matters; provincial affairs; Canadian politics; U.S.-Canadian issues; Canadian Pacific Railway; Indian affairs; military matters; fisheries legislation; policing; shipping; land disputes; elections; official visits; petitions and Fenian threats;

Correspondence and financial papers, c.1871-c.1880, concerning Lord Dufferin's private affairs and the administration of his household;

Speeches, memoranda, pamphlets and newspaper reports, 18 October 1872-c.1904, concerning Lord Dufferin's Governor Generalship of Canada. The speeches include both those made to the Canadian Parliament and to the various institutions he visited whilst on tour. Both British and Canadian newspaper cuttings report on the response to his activities and decisions. Later cuttings include his obituary;

Papers, photographs and drawings, c.1875-5 March 1877, relating to Lord Dufferin's schemes for the improvement of Quebec. They include the work of Belfast architect, W.H. Lynn;

Papers and correspondence, 10 April 1871-c.1877, concerning Lord Dufferin's involvement with the Canadian Pacific Railway and the settlement of British Columbia. Much of this material relates to the Canadian Pacific Railway scandal and the Royal Commission of Inquiry;

Bound volume and memoranda, c.1870-c.1875, concerning Canadian-Indian affairs. The main areas of interest are British Columbia, Manitoba and the North West, with reference being made to missionary work amongst the Mettakertah Indians;

Papers, correspondence and newspaper cuttings, 8 December 1869-November 1874, concerning the civil unrest in the Fort Garry area of Winnipeg. They include the 1869 Declaration of Independence by the French half-breeds and papers concerning the trial of Ambroise Lepine in 1874.
D.1071H/H/1-14

Business papers, 1845-1962, of Blanford Bleachworks Co., Gilford, Co. Down. They include references to trade with Canada.
D.1136

Business papers, 1933-46, of the North of Ireland Linen Co., containing references to trade with Canada.
D.1142

Letter, 13 February 1873, from William Porter, Chebanse, Illinois, to his brother, Ireland, comparing the climates of Canada and the United States in relation to crop production and suggesting that his brother emigrate to the United States.
D.1153/3/25

Extensive letter books, order books etc., January 1906-July 1919, of the Broadway Damask Co., linen mill, Belfast, with references to sales in Kingston, Ontario, in the foreign order book.
D.1193/OF/1

19 letters, 27 June 1849-5 February 1867, from various Canadian correspondents, to Eleanor Wallace, [later McIlrath], in Ireland. 17 letters, 27 June 1849-1860, from Jane White, Goderich, Ontario, form the most important part of this collection as they comment on a wide range of matters including: the voyage from Belfast; the quarantine station at Belle Isle; the first impressions of the country; the celebrations at the fall of Sebastopol; rumours of war with the United States; the Indian way of life; the progress of the railway network; the development of Goderich; railway and steamboat accidents; politics in the locality; the American Civil War; starvation in the Huron area due to crop failure; Fenian unrest; and the development of the local Methodist church. A letter dated 5 February 1867 from William M. White, Goderich, Ontario, refers to the death of Jane White. On 5 July 1858 William Bennett of St George, New Brunswick, wrote to Wallace informing her of attempts to raise funds for the building of a Presbyterian church and asking for her assistance. The final letter in this collection was sent by Wallace in 1853 to a Mrs Clarke, [?], referring to the arrival of friends in 'America' after a perilous journey.
D.1195/3/5, 8B, 9-15, 17-20, 22-5

350 letters, 1931-5, between Robert H. Montgomery, Nova Scotia, and his father, Matthew, Belfast. In addition there are pedigrees of the Montgomery family, Kirkinriola, Co. Antrim, 1830-1960, and the related family of Hanna, Corkey, Co. Antrim, 1760-1960. There is a restricted access to these documents with permission being required from the family.
D.1212

Memorandum book, 1934, kept by Norman Lewis giving details of his monthly wages and expenditure while working as a farm labourer in Ontario. These include the cost of personal items, insurance, stamps and excursions. The book itself is a *Crop Inventory Record and Memo Book* produced by the American Agricultural Chemical Co., and includes advertisements for that Company using Canadian farmers.
D.1218

Copy of an anonymous appeal, 1942, from a Canadian correspondent seeking subscriptions for a church in Canada and describing the poverty in Canada which has led to the lack of funds.
D.1239/12

Legal papers, 1900, concerning the administration of the estate of James Flavelle, Corbrackey, Co. Armagh, and including correspondence and receipts from his relatives in Toronto, Ontario.
D.1251/4/3/1

Two letters, 16-27 June 1832 and c.1845, from J. Woolsey, Quebec, to J.G. Woolsey, Portadown, Co. Armagh. The early letter describes a cholera outbreak in Quebec and a riot in Montreal as well as his business interests. The second letter refers to the treatment of Catholics in Canada *vis a vis* Ireland and the settlement of the New Brunswick-Maine boundary dispute. He also mentions a 'conflagration' in Quebec which has cost him £1000.
D.1252/23/1/2, 9

Autobiographical notes, 1890-1964, of Senator Joseph Cunningham, J.P., Belfast. He was elected Grand Master of the Orange Order of Ireland and visited Canada in this capacity in 1950, leading the Twelfth procession in Toronto, Ontario.
D.1288/1/A-B

Legal papers, 1888-1927, concerning the estates of Annie E.F. Currie, Victoria, British Columbia, and of Isaac Miller, West Garafaxa, Wellington, Ontario. There are also some papers concerning Edward W. Browne's holdings in the Canadian Middle West Trust Co.
D.1326/2/40 and **/18/39, 55**

Legal papers and genealogical material, 1919-45, concerning the following: David Hunter, Keystone, Alberta, who died in August 1922 leaving 160 acres to his beneficiaries in Belfast; James Gibson, Saskatoon, Saskatchewan; and Agnes Wylie, Ballymartin, Templepatrick, Co. Antrim, who died in October 1942 leaving property to relatives in Toronto, Ontario.
D.1349/4/1/1, 5

Letter, 10 July 1858, from Rev. Robert Boyd, Prescott, Canada West, to Robert Young, Ballymena, Co. Antrim, certifying that he is a son of Robert Boyd Snr to enable him to get funds from his father's estate. He also gives details of his life in Canada.
D.1364/B/33

Legal papers, 7 March-26 June 1861, concerning the purchase of shares in the Great Western of Canada Railway Co., by several Ballymena businessmen.
D.1364/I/16

Letter, 13 August 1869, from Col G. Hibbert, Toronto, Ontario, to Captain A.M. Armstrong, 63rd Regiment, Carlisle Fort, Cork, commenting on personal and regimental affairs. He feels that his own regiment will be disbanded soon.
D.1364/J/21D

Copy letter, 14 October 1854, from M.J. Young, Fenaghy, Co. Antrim, to 'My Dear Mary', describing the wreck of the ship *Arctic* off the Newfoundland coast, and the experiences of William Alexander Young and Willie Gihon who were passengers on the ship.
D.1364/J/24

Letter, 27 December 1849, from Rev. Charles Boyd, Ireland, to his son, Henry, Australia, commenting that addresses have been pouring in from all over the world, including Canada, complaining about the removal of the Commission of the Peace from the 3rd Earl of Roden, in Counties Down and Louth.
D.1401/48

Statement of accounts, 1 May 1863-30 April 1864, from E. Haney, Culdaff, Co. Donegal, to James Steele-Nicholson, Canada.
D.1405/77

Letter, 14 May 1884, from J.D. Collins, Peterborough, Ontario, to James Steele-Nicholson, Bangor, Co. Down, giving family news and commenting on the loss of *S.S. Florida en route* from New York to Glasgow, Scotland.
D.1405/82

Diary, visitors' books, addresses and miscellaneous papers, 24 March 1905-16 October 1940, of Lord and Lady Craigavon. The diary belonged to Lady Craigavon and contains an account of the trip she made with her husband, then Sir James Craig, Prime Minister of Northern Ireland, to Canada in 1926. Whilst it is presented as a contemporary diary, it appears likely that there has been some retrospective editing. She includes daily entries beginning on 9 August 1926, when they set sail, and continuing during their voyage and rail journey across Canada. These reminiscences provide a more personal insight to the trip than the official record found at P.M.6/12/3. The visitors' books are for Craigavon, Cleeve Court, Streatley and Glencraig, all homes of Lord Craigavon. There is also a visitors' book for Stormont Castle. All of these include the signatures of various Canadian guests. The miscellaneous papers include an address of welcome to Sir James from the Orangemen and women of Manitoba during his Canadian trip.
D.1415/B/38 pp 168-175, /D/1, 2, 7, 10

1920s newsreel film on Canadian emigrants on board *Orcenta*.
D.1422

Extensive emigrant correspondence, 1815-79, received by Rev. George Kirkpatrick and Rev. A.T. Kirkpatrick, Craigs, Co. Antrim. Their correspondents include: Elizabeth Foster, Quebec and York, Upper Canada, 1815-23; Thomas Kirkpatrick, Kingston, Ontario, 1828; Stafford and George A. Kirkpatrick, Kingston, Ontario, c.1850-1870; Ellen Dunlop, Peterborough, Ontario, c.1875-1889; and Tom A. Hay, Kingston, Ontario, 1877-9. Hay describes a journey to survey townships in Manitoba and Saskatchewan on behalf of the Ottawa and Toronto Railway. There are some 800 letters in this collection and they are unsorted and unlisted at the time of writing.
D.1424/11

Three letters, 4 October 1882-1 October 1889, from Andrew S. Whittell, Barrie, Ontario, to William Hunter, Stewartstown, Co. Tyrone, commenting on various aspects of life in Canada including: his acquisition of property; his work as a fruit farmer and the crop yields he obtains; his appointment as a representative of the Grand Lodge of Good Templars; and other family news. In addition he refers to legacies which are due to him from an Irish source and criticises the Irish solicitors for their tardiness in comparison with their Canadian counterparts.
D.1441/14, 17, 18

Correspondence and accounts, 1902-23, of Strain & Elliot, [later W.J. Strain], linen manufacturers, Bedford St, Belfast. There are some references to contacts in Toronto, Ontario, by the name of Jaselin.
D.1504/1-10

Letters and telegrams, 17 February 1912-25 May 1918, from various Canadian correspondents to Sir Edward Carson, concerning his role as the leader of the anti-Home Rule movement. The correspondents include Sir James Whitney, P.M. and President of the Council of Ontario, who refused to become involved in the Irish situation, and representatives of Orange Lodges in Canada. A letter from Amy Nesbitt, Toronto, Ontario, encloses two postage stamps depicting Carson over the caption 'We will not have Home Rule'. There is also a bundle of telegrams from Canada to Carson expressing sympathy with the position of the Ulster Unionists and opposition to any attempt to coerce Ulster.
D.1507/A/3/11, /A/5/1, /A/21/3-4, /A/23/17-35 and /A/27/10, 16

Extracts, October-December 1859, from the diary kept by J.B. Hamilton, Ballymoney, Co. Antrim, on a voyage to New York, with some passing references to Canada.
D.1518

Folder, 1878-86, of A.H. Dill, Knock, Belfast, containing items relating to lacrosse and including references to matches between Canada and Ireland.
D.1518

Letter, 8 January 1826, from Captain John Boyd, Waterford, Co. Waterford, to John Kane, Belfast, concerning his safe arrival from Quebec and the sale of timber there.
D.1534/1

Legal papers, 1856-95, concerning the estates of William Orr, school teacher, Brock, Ontario, and of Joseph Reid, St John, New Brunswick, and late of Bovevagh, Co. Londonderry.
D.1550/10, 138

Account book, 1886-1905, recording investments on Amherst Island, Ontario, by the Perceval Maxwell family.

Papers, 1774-90, of Colonel John Maxwell, who served on the staff of Sir Guy Carleton, Governor of Quebec, during the American War of Independence. Maxwell also owned land in Quebec and the earliest letter, written from Staten Island, New York, concerns his desire to be back in Canada. There are also six documents relating to Quebec's reaction to the American war and include: a copy of a loyalist address to the king from the French inhabitants of Montreal, September 1774; papers concerning the establishment of a Quebec militia, July and September 1775; and a list of the principal persons settled in the province of Quebec, who served the rebels zealously and fled upon their quitting it, 9 May 1776, and transmitted to Lord George Germain. Two of these documents are in French. There is also a substantial body of papers dealing with Maxwell's financial relations with his estranged wife, including a reference to the provision in his will of the island of Amherst for her even though it was occupied at that time by the troops of the rebellious 13 colonies!
D.1556/7/10, /16/21, /17/2, 4

Diary, 1838, kept by William J. Campbell during a visit to the United States and Canada with descriptions of Montreal, Quebec, St Lawrence, Lake Ontario and Niagara Falls.
D.1558/2/2 pp. 21-44

Copy of the report, November 1938, of the mission to British Columbia by Brigadier General Sir Henry Page Croft and R.S. Dalgliesh 'to investigate the possibilities of community settlement for British immigrants to that Province in August 1938'.
D.1566/2/10

Papers, c.1930-1960, of Professor C.R. Fay, Reader in Economic History at Cambridge University and formerly of the University of Toronto, Ontario. A wide range of topics is covered and many relate to the economic history of Canada, particularly that of Newfoundland and Labrador. These references are scattered throughout and take the form of typescript notes, articles, maps, notebooks, letters and reviews.
D.1571

Journal, March 1786-June 1787, by James O'Bryen on board *H.M.S. Pegasus*, commanded by Prince William Henry. A description is given of the ship's first tour of Newfoundland and Nova Scotia and is presented in the form of standard ship's log entries. The Public Archives of Canada hold another log concerning the same voyage at MG.23 J7).
D.1603

15 letters, 9 December 1829-1895, received by George and Catherine Kirkpatrick, [?], Ireland, from friends and relatives in Canada. Their correspondents include: Thomas Kirkpatrick and E. Rothwell of Kingston, Ontario; Stafford Kirkpatrick, Ellen Dunlop, Anna Hay, Tom Hay and Fanny Stewart, all of Peterborough, Ontario; William Dugan, Nellyburn, Ontario; M. Downsley, Prescott, Ontario; and George B. Kirkpatrick, [?]. The letters cover a wide range of topics including: personal and family affairs; social activities; outbreaks of cholera, smallpox and scarlet fever; unemployment; and missionary work. There are two letters of particular interest. The first of these is from William Dugan, seeking George Kirkpatrick's assistance in bringing his parents to Canada. The other one is from Tom Hay, describing Ontario and Manitoba in glowing terms and suggesting that the need for labour to build the Canadian Pacific Railway offers great possibilities for major Irish emigration to Canada.
D.1604/9, 48, 58, 77, 151, 236, 258, 273, 274, 277, 278, 289, 320, 327, 328

Letter, May 1778, from James Cummyng, Lyon Office, Edinburgh, Scotland, to Sir John Browne of the Neale, Henry Street, Dublin, describing the disappointing response to a circular letter to Nova Scotian baronets suggesting they might subscribe 'for levying men'. A list of the baronets to whom the proposal was sent is also included.
D.1606/1/92

Small disbound volume, March 1806, containing a copy of a memorial sent to the 2nd Earl of Moira, Master General of the Ordnance. The memorial sets out the case of Lt Col Charles Robison, R.A., who had been charged with deserting his post as commandant of the garrison and commanding officer of artillery at St John, New Brunswick, in 1800.
D.1618/16/3

Letter, 8 October 1897, from J.D. Collins, Peterborough, Ontario, to James Steele-Nicholson, Co. Down, describing his journey to Canada and giving family news.
D.1626/15

Manuscript diary, 29 April 1912-28 April 1913, of Lillian Dean (later Lady Spender), covering the period when she was manageress of a dairy belonging to the Hon. Mrs Lionel Guest, on the Isle de St Giles in the St Lawrence river. *En route* to her place of employment she stayed with her uncle and aunt, Sir Ralph Williams and his wife. The diary is a vivid, day by day account of her life in Canada with descriptions of the places she visited and of the people she met, among whom was H.D. Reid, the owner of the Newfoundland Railway. There is also an unbound typescript copy.
D.1633/2/16-18

Memorandum c.1821, from Alexander Lindsay, Trinity College, Dublin, to William Wallace and his son William of Charlotte County, New Brunswick, concerning a lease of lands in Co. Tyrone.
D.1660/4

Letter, 12 June 1842, from Captain William Mitchell, Quebec, to his wife, Londonderry, describing the voyage of the ship of which he was captain and giving details of the number of deaths and births on board. He also comments on the rate of labourers' wages in Canada, noting that '.... the times is very bad [*sic*] in these parts, even worse than in Ireland ....'.
D.1665/1/1

Legal papers, 24 November 1881, concerning the release of Irish lands by James M. Porter, George D. Porter, Andrew Porter and others of Guelph, Ontario.
D.1681/2/1

Plate 1:   Lord Dufferin's scheme for the improvement of Quebec: sketches by the architect W H Lynn, 1875-7. *(PRONI ref. D.1071H/H10/3)*

General View of Citadel with New Chateau St Louis —   *Signed W H Lynn R.H.A. Architect*

Plate 2:   *Lord Dufferin's scheme for the improvement of Quebec: sketches by the architect W H Lynn, 1875-7.*
(PRONI ref. D.1071H/H10/3)

Legal papers, 23 November 1901, concerning the involvement of Elizabeth Corrigan, Toronto, Ontario, in the estate of Sarah Sinclair, Armagh.
D.1696/3

Six letters, 17 April 1832-9 December 1861, received by Rev. Thomas Crawford and his wife, Ireland. The first letter, from Thomas Radcliff, Dublin, refers to a Kitty Elwood going to Canada. The other five letters are from Crawford's sister, Sarah Ann Radcliff, Adelaide, Upper Canada, and describe her life as a settler there. She comments on the rebellion in Lower Canada and requests child apprentices to be sent to her from Ireland. In later life she sought financial assistance as a penniless widow.
D.1700/5/1/10, 11, 14-17

Diary, 1838-41, of James Black, an agent for a cotton trader in North Carolina. The entry for 29 May 1838, written whilst he was on his way home to Ireland, refers to a sighting of the brig *Ann* sailing from London, England to Quebec.
D.1725

Letter, 13 September 1902, from Howard Blizzard, Toronto, Ontario, to Charles Blizzard, Ireland, concerning personal affairs.
D.1751/3/11

Letter, 3 September 1921, from F.C.T. O'Hara, Deputy Minister of the Department of Trade and Commerce, Ottawa, to Ogilvy Graham, York St, Spinning Co., Belfast, concerning the political situation in Ireland and requesting genealogical information. He also comments on a recent visit to Belfast.
D.1754/32

Letter, 7 July 1829, from J. Mulligan, New Brunswick, to his uncle, James Mulligan, Lisnaslegan, Banbridge, Co Down, referring to family news and his disinterest in politics in North America.
D.1757/2/2

Letter, 4 January 1824, from E. Phelps, Moyallen, Co. Down, to Maria Newson, Edenderry, King's Co. Phelps had received a large bundle of letters from 'our dear American wanderers'. [Henrietta, 'sister', Joseph and James] and extracts are quoted from letters 'dated from Kingston, the 9th of November'. These give long, detailed descriptions of a journey which begins at Quebec, moves on to Montreal and Kingston before a boat journey along Lake Ontario to Niagara Falls and a visit to York. Comment is made on the scenery, the people encountered en route, land and commodity prices and the situation where they would most like to settle, with Kingston appearing as the favourite.
D.1762/47

Correspondence, 1930-48, between Fred Wray and others, Toronto, Ontario, and Violet Trench, London, England, concerning research on a Wray family pedigree.
D.1785/1/1/2

Notebook, extract of minutes, pamphlet and letters, 1848-1904, concerning the life and work of the Rev. Alexander McLeod Stavely, who worked as a missionary in New Brunswick and Nova Scotia, having emigrated to Canada from Ulster about 1839/40. He was the principal negotiator when the Presbytery of New Brunswick and Nova Scotia was taken under the jurisdiction of the American synod. Having lost everything in the fire which destroyed much of St John in 1877, he returned to Ireland to raise funds for the rebuilding of the church and remained there until his death. These papers include letters to friends and relatives in Ireland written from St John,

giving details of his surroundings and his work. The notebook contains a handwritten lecture called *The New Hominum. Reflections on Canadian history and failure*. The extract of the minutes of the Presbyterian Church Synod of 1904 and the pamphlet, *The Reformed Witness* of 1903, are tributes to Stavely and contain details of his career in Canada.
D.1792/Section E

Letter book, June 1874-November 1926, of Gaffikin & Co., Bedford St Weaving Co., Ltd, linen manufacturers, Belfast. It includes correspondence with business associates in Montreal, Quebec. The book is in poor condition and is difficult to read.
D.1796/1

Letter, 1 September 1915, from William Carten, Toronto, Ontario, to Miss Grace Carten, Hove, Sussex, concerning a renunciation of claims against property in Whiteabbey, Co. Antrim.
D.1820/1/22

Three letters, 7 June 1838-2 June 1840, from Robert Smith, Philadelphia, Pennsylvania, to James Smith, Moycraig, Co. Antrim. The first two letters discuss the possibility of war between Britain and Canada and between the United States and Canada. There is some reference to Canadian attempts to win support for their cause from Indians. The third letter discusses the boundary question and refers to the dreadful state of emigrants arriving at North American ports, including Quebec. He gives details of the *Independence* which sailed from Liverpool to Quebec with 270 passengers of which 11 died *en route* and 18 had contracted smallpox.
D.1828/8, 15, 18

Manuscript, 1876, entitled *A short history of the emigration and early settlement of the first settlers of the township of Emily, near Toronto*. The period 1690-1876 is covered but the particular focus is on the years after 1819, when the Best family, whose papers these are, emigrated to Emily. There are also typescript genealogical notes relating to the Best family of Newry, Co. Down, and Portadown, Co. Armagh.
D.1846

Two diaries and five photographs, November 1861-January 1864, of Hugh Annesley, 5th Earl of Annesley. The first diary, covering the period November 1861-October 1863 contains details of a voyage on the *Hibernian* from Londonderry to St John, New Brunswick, during the winter and spring of 1862. The second diary, covering the period November 1863-January 1864, describes a hunting trip in Quebec. The scope of both of these is rather limited, although the second contains more information than the first.
D.1854/9/6, 7

The photographs in this collection are as follows:

A young man, possibly a Canadian fur trapper.
D.1854/5/2/11

Hugh Annesley in his Scots Fusilier Guards Captain's uniform whilst on service in Canada.
D.1854/5/7/14

Two hunters equipped with snow shoes etc., portrayed against a snow covered background, with the legend inscribed, 'Col Rhodes, Quebec, equipped for Cariboo'.
D.1854/5/7/44

Horse-drawn sleigh with two military officers, one of whom appears to be Annesley. It was taken on a street in 'Saint John, New Brunswick after a snow fall'.
D.1854/5/7/64

Stuffed head of a bison shot by the 9th Earl of Southesk on 16 July 1859, near the South Saskatchewan river. It is accompanied by a page of manuscript giving details of the kill.
D.1854/5/8/36

Two letters, 8 January 1931, from Mrs M. Spinks and her son, William, Toronto, Ontario, to Miss A.M. Forster, Londonderry, commenting on the high unemployment in Toronto, mainly in the motor industry.
D.1858/6A, B

Letter, 1 July 1832, from John and Eliza Anderson, Quebec, to John Anderson, Coleraine, Co. Londonderry, vividly describing their voyage to Canada and the cholera epidemic which they witnessed in Quebec on their arrival. One of their children died of the disease.
D.1859/1

Letter, 28 April 1911, from Matthew McCaul, on board the *S.S. Ionian*, off Newfoundland, to his father, Londonderry, giving a very detailed account of the events on his voyage to Canada.
D.1893/1

Account book, 1806-20, of Samuel and Andrew McClean and Campbell Graham, Belfast, showing trade in wines and spirits, including carriage and sale, June-October 1814, of goods to Quebec.
D.1905/2/192/1

Ten letters, c.1850, relating to a legal dispute concerning George Saul, a Liverpool shipowner involved in the emigrant trade, and Samuel McCrea, Waring Street, Belfast. The papers include statements of the case, accounts and a reference to the acquirement of shares in the *Constitution*, which was to be used to ship emigrants to New York and Quebec.
D.1905/2/4A

Legal papers, 1911-13, concerning the activities of a Co. Fermanagh based religious sect led by Edward Cooney. The sect had Canadian members and a list of these is included along with reports of the case published in the *Manitoba Free Press*.
D.1906/3-4

Legal papers, 1885, concerning Thomas Stanley, Toronto, Ontario.
D.1929/3/2/6

Letter, 25 March 1878, from John Connor, Mattawa, Ontario, to his wife, Ann, Lurgan, Co. Armagh, concerning legal matters and requesting that if either she or her brother are coming to Canada that they bring flower seeds with them.
D.1929/11/17

Letter, 30 May 1878, from W.J. Jennings, Kendall, Saskatchewan, to his father who is on a trip to Ireland.
D.1930/1

Letter, 14 December 1881, from E.A. Jennings, Toronto, Ontario, to his mother in Ireland giving family news and commenting on crop yields.
D.1930/1

Extensive accounts, ledgers, journals and other papers, 1893-1940, of the Raceview Woollen Mills Ltd, Broughshane, Co. Antrim. Two volumes, 1906-23 and 1922-3, concern the credit-worthiness of customers and have many references to Canadian firms, particularly in Quebec, Montreal and Toronto, Ontario.
D.1933/11/1, 2

Extensive papers, 1901-31, of the Ballygarvey Spinning and Weaving Co., Ballygarvey, Co. Antrim, including a sales ledger, 1908-23, listing sales in Toronto, Ontario, and Montreal, Quebec.
D.1933/16/5

Extensive business papers, 1860-1963, of Henderson & Eadie, woollen manufacturers, Lisbellaw, Co. Fermanagh. These include in-letters, 18 October 1955-16 March 1961, from T. Archer, Toronto, Ontario. Archer was a manufacturer's agent and his first letter proposes that his firm should be allocated an agency for the distribution of Henderson & Eadie's Donegal tweed in Canada. The business relationship develops from there.
D.1938/1/29

Business papers, 1924-47, of Ulster Woollen Mills, Crumlin, Co. Antrim. These include correspondence with Canadian firms.
D.1941

Correspondence, reports, maps, photographs, memoranda and newspaper cuttings, 1914-23, of Lt Col J.W. Boyle. These papers are subdivided into three separate sections: material relating to Boyle's involvement in the 1917-19 Canadian mission to Rumania and Russia; papers concerning the Klondyke Mining Co., Yukon, of which Boyle was president; private correspondence and papers, including miscellaneous items of Canadian interest. The entire archive consists of c.350 documents.
D.1943/1-3

Letter, 25 June 1859, from William George Weir, New York, to Thomas Weir Jnr, [Ireland], concerning details of fellow passengers on board the *City of Baltimore*, and including mention of a Mr McBlain of Newry, Co. Down and Canada.
D.1948/3/8

Legal papers, 16 April 1875, concerning John Smith, of Toronto, Ontario, and of Garvaghy, Co. Tyrone.
D.1957

Extensive business papers, 1921-46, of R. Nelson & Co., Belfast, and an antecedent company, Alexander Boon & Co., Belfast, both of which were handkerchief manufacturers. There are several, scattered references to trade with Montreal, Quebec.
D.2012/1-5

Log books, 1883 and 1885, of voyages made by the barque *Forest Queen* from Belfast to Miramichi Bay, New Brunswick.
D.2015/1/3, 7

Log book, 1882-3, of a voyage made by the barque *Richard Hutchison*, from Sharpness, Gloucestershire to Miramichi, New Brunswick.
D.2015/1/5

Log book, 1885-6, of a voyage made by the *S.S. David Taylor* from Inverness, Scotland, to St John, New Brunswick, and from St John to Belfast.
D.2015/1/8

Ledger account book, 1873, of the expenses of the barques *Granada* and *Forest Queen* on voyages between Belfast and Miramichi, New Brunswick.
D.2015/1/14

Log books, 1880-89, of various ships and their voyages, including some to Canada.
D.2015/1/24

Sea Transport Book, 1936, containing a list of vessels owned by the Lamport Holt Line, with descriptions of some of the ships and places visited, including Canada.
D.2015/2/6

Typescript copies, 1936-55, of broadcast talks by Captain R.H. Davis on Belfast sailing ships, including references to Canadian voyages.
D.2015/3/1

List, 1894-1914, of the voyages of Captain R.H. Davis, including some to Canada.
D.2015/3/5

Miscellaneous shipping papers, c.1870-1890, including a statement of the crew of the *Forest Queen* which was reported to have lost cargo from Miramichi, New Brunswick, to Belfast in 1883.
D.2015/4/1

Letter, 21 September 1963, from Sir George North, Pall Mall, London, to Major General Sir Hugh Tudor, St John's, Newfoundland, requesting information on the life and family history of Miles Clayton, one time Assistant Inspector General of the Royal Irish Constabulary.
D.2022/1/46

Notes and correspondence, 1966, of Dr Donald B. McNeill concerning the ship *Mountjoy II* which was used in the Ulster Volunteers' gun running. McNeill ascertained that it was still in operation on the east coast of Canada under the new name of *Clyde Valley*.
D.2022/3/15

Letter, 20 February 1850, from A. Tyrell, Weston, Ontario, to his sister in Ireland describing his consumptive illness, the weather and his gloomy prospects of finding employment.
D.2068/5

Papers, 19th and 20th centuries, of the Central Council of the Irish Linen Industry, with various references to linen production in Canada.
D.2088

11 letters, 1734-19 April 1748, from Arthur Dobbs, London, England, and Ulster, to Michael and 'Judge' Ward, Dublin, discussing Dobbs's scheme for an expedition to find the North West passage and his attempts to interest the Hudson's Bay Co., in the plan. His progress is outlined in considerable detail including the petitioning of the House of Commons, the opening of a subscription to raise funds, the acquisition of ships, costs, plans for settlement and the possible competition from the Hudson's Bay Co.
D.2092/1/2 p.96, /5/15, /6, 85, 86, 95, 100, 105, 142, 144, 145

Extensive business papers, 1863-1955, of the Old Bleach Linen Co., Randalstown, Co. Antrim, including a Canadian invoice book.
D.2103/5/3

Unlisted Duffin papers containing genealogical notes, correspondence and newspaper cuttings relating to Sir Francis Hincks and his family, Killyleagh, Co. Down, and Belfast. Included is a letter, 15 July 1878, from the 1st Marquess of Dufferin, Governor General of Canada, 1872-8, to Hincks, concerning an article written by the latter referring to the need for the maintenance of constitutional links between Britain and Canada. Dufferin agrees with the sentiments expressed by Hincks.
D.2109

Five letters, 7 August 1887-19 May 1907, from John B. Cherry to his brother, R.R. Cherry in Ireland. J.B. Cherry emigrated to Canada in 1887, settling first at Spencer's Bridge, British Columbia, before moving on to Vancouver, British Columbia. These letters describe his early movements and his unsuccessful attempts to become a barrister in Vancouver. He appears to have been in constant financial trouble and returned to Ireland to take up the post as Registrar and Secretary to his brother who had become Lord Chief Justice of Ireland.
D.2166/1/3/1-5

Legal papers, 1829-90, concerning Hugh Teggart, Wolf Island, Ontario.
D.2223/18/45

Business papers, 1838-1964, of J. & W. Charley & Co., linen manufacturers and bleachers, Dunmurry, Belfast. They include references to trade with Canada.
D.2242

Letters, copy letters, dispatches, memoranda and other miscellaneous papers, 1835-40, of Sir Archibald Acheson, 2nd Earl of Gosford, during his period of service as Governor of Lower Canada, 1835-40. His correspondents include: Lord Glenelg, the Colonial Secretary; Sir John Colborne and Sir Francis Head, successive Lieutenant-Governors of Upper Canada; Sir Colin Campbell, Lieutenant-Governor of Nova Scotia; Sir John Harvey, Lieutenant-Governor of New Brunswick; H.S. Fox, British Minister at Washington; Joseph Hume; Daniel O'Connell; Lord Aylmer; Sir Charles Edward Grey; Lord William Bentinck; Edward Ellice; Lord Dufferin; Lord Westmorland; Lord Devon; and Lord Jocelyn. The papers cover both public and private affairs, including letters of introduction and patronage and words of advice on the Canadian situation. There are also 36 letters from T. Buchanan, 1838-9, writing from the British Consulate at New York, giving news of Canada and of the progress of the Durham mission and reflecting his dispair at the intransigence of the 'Family Compact' in Upper Canada. There is also a memorandum by Lord Gosford of a private meeting he had with Louis Joseph Papineau. Some of this material has been copied by the Public Archives of Canada as MG.11 CO42 and 43.
D.2259/1, /2, /3/1-86, /4/1-37, /5/1-27, /6/1-52, /7/1-34, /8/1-81, /9/1-61, /10/1

Letter, 3 April 1922, from Mrs K.B. Brown, Chicago, Illinois, to Mrs J.L. Payne, Cornwall, Ontario, inquiring as to the whereabouts and welfare of a mutual friend, Robert Haldane.
D.2264/19

Legal papers, 28 February 1895-26 September 1906, concerning Charles Caldwell, Toronto, Ontario, and his involvement in the rental of lands in Ireland.
D.2281/15-19

11 letters, 1848-57, from William Hutton, Montreal and Quebec, to John McCrea Jnr, Leek, Strabane, Co. Tyrone. Hutton was Public Arbitrator, responsible for the settling of disputes about public works in Canada West. He describes his work and gives a glowing account of Canada and his family's life there. The letters refer to his production and publication of an emigrant's guide to Canada and to essays which he wrote on various aspects of Canadian society. He offers his assistance to McCrea's son if he wishes to emigrate. Other references include mention of George Stephenson's trip to Canada to construct a bridge over the St Lawrence and a description of a tour of Niagara Falls.
D.2298/4/2

Business papers, 1910-60, of Samuel McCrudden & Co., Ltd, linen manufacturers, Belfast, and including references to trade with Canada.
D.2306

Four letters, 29 December 1941-25 April 1949, from Robert Jefferson, Bishop of Ottawa, to his mother and sister in Ireland, describing his episcopal duties and commenting on the visits of Winston Churchill and the Archbishop of York to Ottawa.
D.2409/1-4

Business papers, 1883-1951, of Glendinning, McLeish & Co., linen manufacturers, Belfast, including references to trade with Canada.
D.2424

43 letters, 1838-42, from Alexander Caledon, who became the 3rd Earl of Caledon in 1839. They are mainly written from the barracks at Quebec, but also include a description of a tour by canoe as far as the Red River with Sir George Simpson, Governor of the Hudson's Bay Co., and then on to join a buffalo hunt on the Plains, ending at St Peter, Minnesota.
D.2433/B/8/1-43

Correspondence, 1842-70, of W.J. Alexander and E.J. Alexander, legal advisors of the Caledon family, concerning the Canadian assets and debts of the 3rd Earl. The former consists of shares in the Marmora Mining Co., and the latter of an apparently fradulent demand of one James Moty of Quebec against the late Earl.
D.2433/B/20/1-64

Journals, 1879-1895, of the 4th Earl of Caledon during a series of hunting expeditions in North America. Included are: a diary, original and photocopy, of a hunting trip in the Bighorn Mountains, entering and leaving through Canada in 1880; similar, of a hunting trip progressing *via* Thunder Bay to Poplar Point, Saskatchewan, and into the Kewatin District in 1883; similar, of a hunting expedition to the Upper Ottawa River as far as Little Lake and a second account of a trip up the Mattawa River, both in 1886; and similar, of a hunting expedition into the American West in 1888, with a few passing references to Canada. These diaries are about 200 pp in length and give detailed descriptions of the hunting, the topography and of the native life. There is also a list, c.1895, of trophies and museum pieces some of which were probably acquired on these trips.
D.2433/B/23/1-8

Six of a set of seven printed plans of the St Lawrence river below Quebec. They were produced by the Hydrographical Office of the Admiralty in 1837.
D.2433/B/25/7-12

Volume, 1838-42, of 22 large format watercolours and one pencil drawing made during the 3rd Earl's Canadian posting. The subjects are military and daily life in Quebec and winter hunting scenes, probably in central Canada. There are also colour slide copies of some of the water colours.
D.2433/B/25/13-14

Business papers, 1860-68, of Downpatrick Timber, Slate & Coal Co., Ltd, including references to trade with Canada.
D.2437

Manuscript autobiography, 1837-96, of Miss E.S. Raynes describing a journey from Ireland to Canada on an emigrant ship in 1850.
D.2452/2

Copy conveyance and draft deed, 20 January and 20 June 1778, involving 480 acres of the townland of Ballybranagh, Co. Down, to which Henry Caldwell of Quebec is a party.
D.2480/2/14, 15

Three letters, 2-17 August 1891, from Bob [?], to his mother in Ireland. He was writing whilst on holiday in Canada and the letters were sent from: Kingston, Ontario; Siccanious, British Columbia; and 'on board a steamer' on the Great Lakes. There are also two sheets of note paper giving details of a hunting trip he made to the Rockies between 20 August-29 September 1891.
D.2480/6/3

Books of newspaper cuttings, March 1926-April 1954, relating to the Ulster Branch of the Overseas League, with references to links with Canada.
D.2496/4-5

Letter and visiting card, 7 January 1929, from Joshua Cooper O'Beirne, Toronto, Ontario, to Captain Cornelius O'Beirne, Royal Ulster Constabulary, Belfast, reminding him that he has not replied to his letter in which he was enquiring about his father who left Longford town about the year 1832-3. He gives details of his father's life.
D.2515/5, 8

Four photographs, c.1890-c.1929, of Mary Jane, Eliza and Robert Hamilton, [?], Ontario, and Esther Albin of Albany, Ontario.
D.2522/1-4

Typescript history, c.1700-c.1920, of the related families of Meighen and McClenaghan, Bovevagh parish, Co. Londonderry, and Drummond and Perth, Ontario.
D.2547/34

Business papers, 1908-71, of Joseph Morton Ltd, wholesale seed merchants, Banbridge, Co. Down, with references to trade with Canada.
D.2550

Testamentary papers, 1903 and 1945, of George F. Greeves, Arthur, Manitoba, and of William Bolton, Kilrea, Co. Londonderry. Greeves had lived in Canada for 18 years, having left England a bankrupt. Bolton had Canadian beneficiaries, including a Mrs Hill of Toronto, Ontario.
D.2587/2/51, 64

Legal papers, 1831-76, concerning the property and estate of the Knox family of Rush Brook, Co. Londonderry and of Canada. Some members of the family owned land at St Pierre, Montreal, Quebec. References to an abbatoir are included.
D.2587/8/1, 3

Advertising posters, c.1900, of shipping lines, including, one for the Canadian Pacific line stating that 'Canada wants farmers'.
D.2607

Unproved will, 8 May 1891, of Florence P. Marshall of Strabane, Co. Tyrone. The legatees are Catherine Marshall Porter of Guelph, Ontario, and Margaret Ellen Marshall of Massagaweys, Ontario.
D.2609/3/22

Letter, 28 March 1857, from John Miller, Hamilton, Ontario, to Susan Maguire, Drumallen, Co. Down, referring to his chance reunion with his older sister and his employment with the Great Western Railway.
D.2630/2/7

Business papers, 1877-1965, of William Clarke & Sons, linen manufacturers, Upperlands, Co. Londonderry, including references to trade with Canada.
D.2659

Four letters, 1 March 1909-6 April 1911, from [Sam?] in Berryland, Ontario; St Mary's, Ontario; and Regina, Saskatchewan, to 'Nick' in Ireland describing his job in Berryland, encouraging him to emigrate to Canada and advising him as to what to bring in clothes and money. He refers to a large influx of immigrants to Regina and suggests that it would be a good place to settle in the future.
D.2709/1/69, 70, 72, 74

Letter, June 1912, from S. McIlroy, Toronto, Ontario, to Mr Shanks, [Ireland], describing Toronto and praising its architecture, especially the churches.
D.2709/1/75

Letter, undated, from John Shanks, Chicago, Illinois, to his unnamed cousin in Ireland, concerning a journey to Canada with wheat *via* the locks of the St Lawrence canal. Other letters in this series deal with shipping on the Great Lakes but do so from the American side.
D.2709/1/86

Letter, 13 December 1812, from Charles Martin, U.S.A., to his brother, Ebeneezer Martin, Ballooly, Co. Down, referring to '.... very trouble sam times. Here they are busy fighting on the lines betwixt the Unighted states and Canidy [*sic*] ...'.
D.2722/5

Letter, 19 July 1853, from Farnworth & Jardine of Liverpool, England, to Captain Samuel Smiley of the *Lady Russell* giving instructions for the delivery of a cargo of salt to St John's, Newfoundland.
D.2723/1/13

Letter, 22 June 1854, from [?] Smiley, Philadelphia, U.S.A., to Captain Samuel Smiley, *Lady Russell* at Quebec, praising Smiley on his speed at crossing the Atlantic and the lack of sickness among passengers. He also refers to the movements of other ships.
D.2723/1/16

Letter, 14 August 1854, from Samuel Smiley, Liverpool, England to his brother, Thomas, Islandmagee, Co. Antrim, concerning the passenger ship *Origora* going to Quebec with a full complement of passengers and the expected arrival of two ships from Quebec at Liverpool.
D.2723/1/17

Letter, 22 July 1856, from Samuel Smiley, on the *Lady Russell* to his brother Thomas stating that he has received orders to go to Quebec and will not be able to visit Ireland for 3 or 4 months. He had been employed in government service, transporting troops and supplies during the Crimean war.
D.2723/1/34

Commonplace book, c.1862-1879 of Alexander Matthews, Portstewart, Co. Londonderry. It includes references to emigrants to Canada, including his own brother and daughter who went to New Brunswick.
D.2738/5/6

Visitors' book, 2 December 1904-11 June 1917, of the Ulster Club, Belfast, and including names of Canadian visitors.
D.2744/M2/1

Letter, 15 August 1909, from Thomas Cameron, railway clerk, Winnipeg, Manitoba, to Annie Cameron, Coleraine, Co. Londonderry, concerning legal matters.
D.2767/36

Letter, 12 January 1869, from the 5th Earl Spencer, Lord Lieutenant of Ireland, Harleston, North-ampton, to Thomas O'Hagan, Lord Chancellor of Ireland, [Ireland], referring to the effects the release of Fenian prisoners in Ireland would have on the actions of Fenians in the United States against Canada.
D.2777/8/7

Typescript of a journal, 1869-70, by Thomas Workman, describing a voyage on the *S.S. Nestorian* from Londonderry to Canada and his travels in Canada and the eastern and south-ern States of America. He travelled from Portland, Maine, through Montreal, Ottawa, Toronto, Niagara Falls, Paris, Windsor to Detroit. He describes the reception of Prince Arthur in Canada. The journal is illustrated with contemporary photographs and with watercolour sketches which appear to have been cut from letters. The photographs are of the Chaudiere Falls and Niagara Falls whilst the sketches include a cariole, tobogganing, a view of Rideau Falls and an excellent view of a derailed train 15 miles beyond Collingwood, travelling from Toronto.
D.2778/1/1A-B

Journal, 1854-5, of the *Lady Russell* by Captain Samuel Smiley, including voyages from Liver-pool to Quebec *via* Tralee, 3 May-16 June 1854 with 490 emigrant passengers, and Quebec to Liverpool, 13 July-11 August 1854. **D.2784/6**

Legal papers, 1937-49, concerning the estates of: Robert Hood, Nebraska; of Sarah Rogers, Toronto, Ontario, and of J. McKay, Saskatchewan. All of these people held property in Canada or passed it on to Canadian relatives.
D.2792/3/1, 2

Detailed manuscript report, 1925-9, of Harford H. Montgomery's world-wide investigations for insurance companies. His work included estimating fire loss and valuing property with New-foundland being amongst the places he visited.
D.2794/5/6

Letter, 24 October 1911, from William Donnan, Toronto, Ontario, to his father Hugh, Co. Down, giving a detailed account of his journey west across Canada. He went by rail from Toronto to Carberry, Manitoba, where he worked during the harvest time before returning to Toronto for the winter.
D.2795/5/3

Business papers, 1860-1960, of Harland & Wolff, shipbuilders, Belfast, and including references to contracts with Canadian firms.
D.2805

Four letters, c.June-August 1867, from John White to his mother, Ireland. The first letter was written just as he was about to leave Londonderry for Canada on board the *Nestorian*. The second letter, written from on board the ship in the St Lawrence, describes the voyage and his fellow passengers, many of whom were French-Canadians. The other letters deal with his travels and observations in Quebec.
D.2861/E/4-6, 14

Three volumes of passenger lists, February 1847-1849, February 1850-August 1857, March 1858-July 1867, of J. & J. Cooke, shipping agents, Londonderry. The Canadian destina-tions are Quebec and St John, New Brunswick, with details also being given for Philadephia and New Orleans. The information recorded includes: details of the ships involved; date of sailing; names of agents employed in Ireland; commissions they received; lists of cancellations; total numbers of passengers carried; and the names, addresses and ages of the passengers. There are

also references to special circumstances, such as the numbers of passengers paid for by landlords or of emigrants sent from the workhouses. There are 723 pages in total.
D.2892/1/1-3

Copy out-letter book, 6 January 1837-27 March 1847, of John Cooke, later J. & J. Cooke, including letters to Quebec and St John, New Brunswick, relating to the Canadian timber and emigrant trade. Great detail is provided of the business and financial transactions involved including: the purchasing of vessels; preparations for voyages; purchase of provisions; and the fitting out of ships. Canadian correspondents include Samuel Thompson and Thomas Wallace, St John, and Messrs Lemessurier, Tilstone & Co., Quebec. Lists are also provided of the ship owners and of their captains and some details are given of ships which Cooke had built at St John.
D.2892/2/1

Copy out-letter book, 24 April 1826-18 October 1834, of William McCorkell & Co., shipping agent, Londonderry, concerning timber cargoes and the emigrant trade. Reference is made to the rate of fares and to the arrangement of insurance for the vessels. Letters of instruction to the captains and masters are included. The Canadian correspondents are Hugh Johnston and John R. Partelow, St John, and William Pentland, Quebec. *(See also* T.2511).
D.2892/2/2

Photographs, mostly undated, of advertising posters and sailing ships, including many references to Canada.
D.2892/4/1-14

Four boxes of unsorted papers, c.1830-c.1965, of the Cooke family. Amongst these papers is the material gathered by T.S.F. Cooke during the research for his book, *The Maiden City and the Western Ocean*. These include a plethora of data on the ships involved in the emigrant trade with Canada and on the administration of the J. & J. Cooke shipping line itself.
D.2892/6

Letter, 20 July 1917, from Thomas Aloysius Whyte, France, to his mother, Loughbrickland, Co. Down, commenting on the activities of the Canadian Corps in France during the 1st World War.
D.2918/7/E/23

Letter, June 1820, from Charles Wilson, Quebec, to James Harper, Belfast. Wilson, a provisions and general merchant in Belfast, was on a business trip and sent news of commercial conditions.
D.2934/1/7

Letter book, 28 March 1828-12 April 1831, of Edward Keogh, merchant, New Ross, Co. Wexford which includes correspondence with William Kydd, St John, Newfoundland relating to the importation of fish from Newfoundland.
D.2935/5

Four letters, 1955-9; received by John Marshall, Windsor, Ontario. His correspondents included: R.L. Marshall, Prehen, Co. Londonderry; W.F. Marshall, The Manse, Castlerock, Co. Londonderry; Bernard Colton, Tattysallagh, Omagh, Co. Tyrone; and Thomas McElhill, Tattysallagh, Omagh, Co. Tyrone. They discuss family history and comment on the oral traditions and the purchase of farms in the early part of the 20th century.
D.2943/1-4

Printed circular postcard, 12 February 1915, produced by Henderson Bros Ltd, Londonderry, and sent to emigration agents in Ireland. It advertised the ships of the Anchor Line which sailed to North America. In this case it had been sent to T. Irvine Graham, Aughnacloy, Co. Tyrone.
D.2948/2/2

Printed maps, 1838, of Upper and Lower Canada, published by J. Arrowsmith, London.
D.2966/35/3-4

Letter, 17 June 1852, from [?], Sherbrooke, Quebec, to 'Dear uncles and aunts', [Ireland], describing the voyage to Canada and the reception given to emigrants. Details are given of illness in the family and of the conditions in the quarantine station. They moved on from Quebec to St Francis by steamboat.
D.2967/3

Biography of John Work, native of Donegal, who emigrated to Canada in 1814 and subsequently became an employee of the Hudson's Bay Company, 1825-55.
D.2980 add

Pedigree, c.1600-1920, of the Macoun family of Lurgan and Portadown, Co. Armagh and Ottawa, Canada.
D.3000/2/1

Typescript genealogical account, 1820-1930, of the ancestors and descendants of George Washington Stone, Dunham, Quebec, and of William Allan Arthur, Vermont, U.S.A., up to the birth of his grandson, Chester Allan Arthur, 21st President of the United States.
D.3000/19/1

Copy pedigree, compiled in 1920 and covering the period 1769-1917, of the related families of: Scott and Hull, Moira, Co. Down; Drogheda, Co. Louth; and Montreal, Quebec.
D.3000/61

Two pedigrees, 17th century-1967, of various related families, including the Morrison family of Enniskillen, Co. Fermanagh and Ontario.
D.3000/63/2

Pedigree, compiled in 1981 and covering the period 1859-1981, of the Emmerson family who emigrated from Co. Down to Ontario.
D.3000/67

Typescript genealogical notes and pedigree, compiled in 1970 and covering the period 1808-1953, relating to the McGreer family of Cushendall, Co. Antrim, Lake County, California and Napanee, Ontario.
D.3000/68

Genealogical papers and a printed book, c.1500-c.1900, relating to the McCurdy family of various locations in the United States and Canada. The author of the book is H.P. Blanchard and it is entitled *Genealogical Record and Biographical Sketches of the McCurdy's of Nova Scotia*, 1930.
D.3000/70/1-3

Booklet of genealogical notes, compiled in 1982 and covering the period 1810-1981, concerning the Smith family of Seskinore and Omagh, Co. Tyrone, Belfast and Ontario.
D.3000/72

Typescript genealogical notes, compiled in 1983 and covering the period 1795-1980, concerning the Crozier family of Newtownhamilton, Co. Armagh, Castleblayney, Co. Monaghan, and Ontario.
D.3000/81

Genealogical notes and pedigree, 1830-1979, relating to the Espie/Espey family of Dungannon and Cookstown, Co. Tyrone, Portadown, Co. Armagh, and Toronto, Ontario.
D.3000/82

Typed transcripts, compiled in 1984, of notices which appeared in Canadian local newspapers, mostly the *New Brunswick Courier*, 1830-46, and the *Toronto Irish Canadian*, 1869. The notices include queries as to the whereabouts of various persons who had emigrated from Ulster to Canada and the United States.
D.3000/104/1-10

Typed transcripts, compiled 1984-5, of notices inserted in Canadian local newspapers by passengers arriving from Ireland. The newspapers were the *New Brunswick Courier* and the *Saint John Morning News*, covering the period 1828-58. There are also summaries based upon these notices which list the passengers involved, their ports of embarkation in Ireland and the dates of arrival in Canada.
D.3000/104/11-13

Pedigree, c.1800-1984, of the Glinton/Glenfield family of Ballymaglave North, Cargacreevy, Dromara and Cabragh in Hillsborough parish, all in Co. Down, Belfast, Portpatrick, Scotland, Montreal, Quebec and New Orleans.
D.3000/105/2

Genealogical notes, c.1732-1984, relating mainly to the allied families of Garrett, Lennox and Foster of Magherafelt, Co. Londonderry, Australia, U.S.A., and Canada.
D.3000/106

Genealogical notes and letters, 17th century-c.1980, relating to the Carrothers family of London, Westminster and Toronto, Ontario, Vancouver, British Columbia, and Edmonton, Alberta. They examine the Canadian movements of the Carrothers family in considerable detail. The letters were written by R.O. Montgomery of Vancouver between 1922 and 1931. He sought information on the family history from various members in Ireland and Canada.
D.3000/110

Typescript, compiled July 1986, entitled 'In search of the Peels and Braidens', by Bruce Braden Peel. It traces the genealogical history of the Peel family of Kiffaugh, Co. Cavan, from 1649 to 1845 and latterly from 1845 to 1946 when a branch of the family resided in Manvers township, Durham County, Ontario. It also traces the history of the Braden family of Marshall, Co. Cavan and latterly of Cartwright township, Durham County, Canada from c.1820 to 1874.
D.3000/128

Journal, 26 July 1890, of Sir Victor Brooke's North American tour. He travelled from Montreal to Vancouver *via* Jackfish, Savanna, Winnipeg, Calgary and Banff. From Vancouver he made a trip into the United States. He also visited Niagara Falls before returning home from New York. His account contains many personal observations including expressing an intention to purchase land around Calgary. Brooke was particularly impressed by the abundance of game for hunting which he found in Canada.
D.3004/D/28

Folder of newspaper cuttings, April-May 1950, containing cuttings relating to the tour of the United States and Canada by Sir Basil Brooke, Prime Minister of Northern Ireland.
D.3004/E/28

Pedigree, compiled in 1966, of the Wilson family of Port Hope, Ontario.
D.3014/2/10

Copy letter, 1967, from Jack F. Douglas, Port Hope, Ontario, to Professor T.B.W. Reid, Oxford, England, relating to the genealogy of the Reid family.
D.3014/2/14

Eight letters, 1910-28, from Robert Reid, Montreal, Quebec, to his father and brother, Armagh, describing his employment in a Montreal store and the prosperity of the city. He comments on the enterprising spirit of the citizens and the large number of Presbyterian churches in the city. Reference is also made to the heatwave during the summer of 1911 which, he says, led to many deaths. In the later letter to his brother he mentions his illness and discusses the medical services in Montreal.
D.3014/3/8/8-15

18 volumes, 1797-1846, of letterbooks, invoice books, sales books, ledgers and other papers, of James McClenaghan, merchant, of Merchants' Quay, Newry, Co. Down. These volumes record the daily transactions of business including the importation of dried fish, iron and cod oil from Newfoundland. The following are of particular interest: three letterbooks, February 1821-February 1846, which contain the firm's out-letters, including those to St John's, Newfoundland, and to merchants and retailers in its own hinterland concerning goods received; three volumes, July 1818-March 1828, containing details of individual consignments imported to and exported from Newry, with entries on the types of materials, their weight, cost and port of shipment; three volumes, March 1825-May 1931, containing details on the sale locally of the imports, with entries on the types of materials, their weight, cost and to whom they were sold; two volumes, August 1820-October 1837, containing details of sales and purchases of goods, both local and foreign; volume, 1797-1824, containing details of transactions with merchants to whom exports were shipped and from whom materials were imported. Reference is also made to the local businessmen who purchased the goods on arrival at Newry.
D.3025A/1/1-3, /2/1-3, /3/1-3, /5/1-2 and /7/1

Papers of Robert Stewart, Viscount Castlereagh, and 2nd Marquess of Londonderry, (1769-1822). The offices he held included Secretary of State for War and the Colonies, 1805-06 and 1807-09, and Secretary of State for Foreign Affairs, 1812-22. The papers of interest refer to Castlereagh's general involvement with North American affairs and in particular with his responsibility for Canada as Colonial Secretary. Most of the material is concerned with military and defence matters but there is some reference to supplying British Government dockyards with timber from Quebec and the maintenance of the Newfoundland fisheries. There are also papers dealing with the 1812 war, including passing references to Canada.
D.3030/2190, 2311, 2316, 2553, 2556, 2572, 2591, 2592, 3366, 3983, 3997, 4022, 4287, 4291 and D1-5

Papers of Sir Robert Henry Meade, who served as private secretary to the 2nd Earl of Granville at the Colonial Office, 1868-71, and as Permanent Under-Secretary for the Colonies, 1892-7. They include an undated note from Meade to Granville and the 1st Earl of Kimberley concerning the Hudson's Bay Co.
D.3044/J/371

Family history, 1927-65, of the Gages of Ontario.
D.3045/4/7

Diary, correspondence and printed article, 18 April 1833-1982, relating to the Young family of Guelph, Ontario. The diary was kept by Brooke Young during his voyage to Quebec on board the ship *Ariadne*, and the correspondence relates to their early life as settlers on Culdaff Farm. There are descriptions of the legal arrangements surrounding land grants, his building work and news of other immigrants, with details of his role as an employer for them. The printed article, by Edgar Vaughan, and entitled *The Cousins Brooke Young and George Harvey in Historic Guelph, the Royal City* was published in *Guelph Historical Society Journal, Ontario*, vol. 20, April 1981.
D.3045/4/13, /6/8, /7/5/1

Business papers, 1838-1961, of J.P. Corry & Co., Ltd, timber merchants, Belfast, and including references to trade with Canada.
D.3051

Volume of postcards, 5 June 1905, including some views of Canada. They were formerly in the possession of Miss Elsie McIlroy, Belfast.
D.3098

Three letters, 1929-31, concerning the possibility of the 7th Marquess of Londonderry becoming Governor General of Canada. The first letter, from Robert Lynn, Washington, U.S.A., suggested that this would be a fitting post for Londonderry. The other letters concern the offer made to him in 1931, and his rejection of it. They were both written by Baron Stamfordham, George V's Private Secretary.
D.3099/2/4, 11

Five letters, 1911, to Maureen Vane-Tempest Stewart, [Ireland], from her father, the 7th Marquess of Londonderry, written whilst he was on a trip to Canada. This is closed to the public until 2012.
D.3099/13/4

Two letters, 18 September 1830, (written on the same piece of paper), from Mrs Frances Adams, South River, Ontario, to her brothers-in-law, David and Robert Adams, Ballymena, Co. Antrim. The first, to David, tells of her son's purchase of land and comments on the price of crops and livestock. She also gives news of other immigrants. The second letter, to Robert, advises him of the advantages of emigrating to Ontario.
D.3104/1/1A-B

Ledgers, accounts, minutes, photographs, letters and other papers, 1870-1969, of the Ulster Steamship Co., and G. Heyn & Sons Ltd, and their subsidiaries. These extensive papers give a wide range of information on all the companies affairs including details of dates of passages, of the cargoes and passengers carried and of the expenses and profits involved. Amongst the many photographs of the lines' ships taken in Canadian waters are those of the *Carrigan Head* celebrating the ship's first entering Montreal, Quebec, after the winter thaw in Canadian Centenary Year. There is also a letter, 1938, from a satisfied passenger who travelled from Greenock, Scotland to Montreal with the Head Line.
D.3117

Business papers, 1865-1961, of S. McCausland Ltd, seed merchants, Belfast, including references to trade with Canada.
D.3136

Coloured poster, 20th century, advertising the ships of the Cunard Line which were sailing between Ireland and North America. Fares and embarkation times are given.
D.3148

Journal, 1760-70 by John Moore of Carrickfergus, Co. Antrim, chronicling his life in the U.S.A.. He emigrated in 1760 and worked for a period, August-November 1761, for his uncle who was a sutler with the British Army at Crown Point, New York State. Moore describes the British movements up Lake Champlain and the Richelieu River to Montreal, Quebec, in 1760 and the fall of Ile Aux Noix and Sorel. He also comments on his work, the conditions of the soldiers and the state of the forts along Lake Champlain. He contrasts the French and English treatment of native peoples and makes some acute observations on American life. The latter part of the diary (after p.86) concerns his return to Ireland.
D.3165/2/1

Business papers, 1911-53, of Harry Ferguson Motors Ltd, Belfast. They include references to the possibility of finding a base in Canada for the world wide distribution of the firm's agricultural machinery. There is also correspondence with the Sun Life Assurance Co., of Canada.
D.3212

25 letters, 1813-39, to Samuel Omay from various literary figures in Scotland and England. The principal correspondent is the Scottish novelist, John Galt. Galt was the Canada Company's superintendent in Upper Canada and played a leading role in the founding of Guelph. His letters to Omay comment on his business interests in Canada and later upon his dismissal from office after quarelling with the Lieutenant Governor, Sir Peregrine Maitland, in 1829. Internal evidence suggests that Galt's letters from Upper Canada, which originally accompanied this group, have been deposited in the Archives of Ontario.
D.3220/1/8-33

Notes, 11 February 1862, by James Coates, Eastwood, Ontario, on the death of Ensign Huey of the 103rd Regiment in the assault on Fort Erie, Niagara, 14 August 1814.
D.3220/2/6

Diary and letters, 1830-40, of Henry Tyler. The letters refer to a proposed trip to Canada and to the trip itself, including some sent from Toronto, Ontario, and Montreal, Quebec. The diary gives a more detailed account of the journey, August 1836-November 1837. He travelled from Niagara to Montreal before spending some time hunting in the vicinities of Trafalgar township and Barrie, Ontario. He comments on the life of a gentleman in the wilds.
D.3220/4/3A pp. 124-45, /4/4, 34

Journal, 1836, kept by Thomas Cather during a trip to North America, with scanty references to Canada. This was printed under the title, *Thomas Cather's Journal of a Voyage to America in 1836*, (London, 1955).
D.3220/5/16-18

13 letters, 1921-3, from Catherine Tyler to Sir Henry Macdonald Tyler, [?], describing her life and travels in Ontario and Saskatchewan.
D.3220/10/1151-63

Two letters, 3 October [?]-5 March 1859, from William Perceval, Wolf Island and Amherst Island, Ontario, to his uncle, J.W. Maxwell Jnr, [?], Ireland, describing his surroundings and discussing personal and financial matters.
D.3244/F/12/5, 10

Certificates and 22 log books, 1886-1968, of the merchant ship, *Clyde Valley*. Some of the certificates were issued in Nova Scotia and the logs record the ship's working life, much of it being spent in the waters of eastern Canada.
D.3251

Two letters and two photographs, 1939-42, from Norman Hanna, Montreal, Quebec, to his mother, Bangor, Co. Down. The first letter describes his rescue following the sinking of the *Athenia* by a submarine and gives news of his plans to join his brother who is working for the Anglo-American Oil Co. The second letter explains his reasons for joining the Royal Canadian Air Force and the photographs show him in his uniform.
D.3265/1, 2 and 3A-B

Seven letters, 23 March 1857-28 April 1878, from William and Malcolm Gamble, St George, New Brunswick, to their family, Magherascouse, Co. Down, concerning their fortunes as immigrants in Canada. The letters give family news and describe their work as loggers and lime burners. William owned 25 acres and he comments on how he farmed it and his success in local agricultural shows. Lists of prices are also provided.
D.3305/1/3, 6, 9-11, 13, 23

Letter, 7 October 1876, from James Gamble, California, to his cousin, Sarah, Ireland, referring to an unprofitable working trip he made to the mines of British Columbia.
D.3305/1/21

Letter, 30 November 1977, from Peter Gibson, Calgary, Alberta, to Annie Roycroft, Bangor, Co. Down, referring to his life as a journalist.
D.3305/5/4

Business papers, 1936-51, of Alexander Finlay Ltd, soap, candle and glycerine manufacturers, Belfast, including references to trade with Canada.
D.3341

Two journals, 1852 and 1854, kept by Charles Denton during tours of North America. They include detailed descriptions of his travels in Canada.
D.3366/D/2 & 4

Photograph, c.1900, of Main Street, Strabane, Co. Tyrone, showing the Emigration Office.
D.3374/1

Postcard album, c.1900-1917, containing some views of Canada.
D.3473

Three letters, 22 June 1863-10 November 1869, from James Collins, Peterborough, Ontario, to relatives in Donegal, Ireland. He requests two young men to be sent to him to help him on his farm and gives family news. He also complains that the £10 sent to him by a relative to fund his trip to Ireland would not even take him to the sea from where he lived.
D.3513/1/22, 23, 27

Account of a voyage, 3 September [c.1850], written "off the Banks of Newfoundland". No departure points or destinations are given.
D.3513/1/49

Plan, c.1880, of the nine townships in the county of Peterborough, Ontario, which were the property of the Canadian Land and Emigration Co.
D.3513/6/4

Three boxes, c.1830-50, of unsorted material relating to the Shirley estate in the western half of the barony of Farney, Co. Monaghan. Much of this refers to the estate management of Evelyn John and Evelyn Philip Shirley and their agents but there is also material concerning the

emigration of Shirley tenants to Canada, the United States and Australia. This includes bundles of petitions from tenants who want to emigrate and are seeking assistance from the landlords. The correspondence of the Shirleys and their agents details the availability of ships and the cost of provisions along with lists of those who were to be offered assistance and the allowance which they received. There are also printed vouchers for the emigrants which contain their names, ages, townland of origin, date of departure and the allowance they were paid. However, no details are given as to the destinations of these people.
D.3531/P/Boxes 1-3

Six letters, 17 May 1830-29 May 1832, from Crofton Thomas Vandeleur to his mother, [Ireland]. Vandeleur was writing from various barracks in Canada including: Fort Monkton, New Brunswick; Cork and Buttevant, Halifax, Nova Scotia; and Annapolis Royal. He describes his activities in the British Army.
D.3549/A/2/8-13

Journal, 1830-31, kept by Crofton Thomas Vandeleur during a voyage to St John's, Newfoundland, in 1830.
D.3549/A/4/11

Letter, 4 November 1867, from James Murphy, c/o James R. Moore, St Mary's, Ontario, to his sister Eliza, Belfast, giving family news.
D.3558/1/3

c.1500 documents. Papers of the late Professor E.R.R. Green, Belfast. Collected during Green's lifetime, 1935-82, they contain originals and copies of emigrant letters, including some from Canada. They also include genealogical material, research notes, printed works and correspondence concerning the Professor's information gathering in Canada. Most of the letters have been copied and are referred to under a separate listing elsewhere in this catalogue.
D.3561

Embarkation return, 4 June 1815, for the 89th Regiment of Foot at Quebec.
D.3574/A/2/6

Journal, correspondence and official papers, 1839-72, of William Power. Power made a journey to the United States and Canada in 1839 and he kept a journal of his travels, including mention of a visit to Montreal, Quebec, and St John, New Brunswick. In later life he had a distinguished military career, spent mainly in the Commissariat department. He served in Canada in the 1860s and the official papers relate to his duties as Commissary General in charge of the Treasury Chest, Canada. His correspondence during this period comprises personal letters to his wife and a series of letters describing his duties to a Foreign Office official known only as 'My Dear FitzWatt'. There is also an undated draft or copy letter to *The Daily News* concerning the maintenance of constitutional links between Britain and Canada.
D.3585/A/3/35, 36, /B/2/67, 69, 70, /B/3/9-41, /B/7/4 and /B/8/3

Two boxes containing c.500 unsorted and unlisted letters, 19th century. They include letters to Mrs C.H. Higginson, Cushendun, Co. Antrim, from her sons who were serving in the army abroad. Among these are letters from Charles Henry Barkley Higginson, who died in Calgary, Alberta, whilst serving with the 1st Battalion of the Royal Dublin Fusiliers. He was on a visit to his sister, Mrs Walter Skrine, at the time of his death.

c.50 letters, 1894-8, from Agnes Skrine, High River, Alberta, to her mother Mrs. C.H. Higginson and various other members of her family in Ireland, describing her life as a rancher's wife.
D.3590/K, L, M

Letter, 1 April 1809, from John O'Raw, Charleston, South Carolina, to his father and mother in Ireland referring to a mutual friend, Thomas Boyd, who had gone home to Ireland leaving his brother alone in Halifax, Nova Scotia.
D.3613/1/2

Correspondence and papers, c.1850-1890, of Vere Foster, a supporter of assisted emigration from Ireland. These papers cover the various aspects of his work to improve the availability and quality of assistance and include: advice from correspondents in Canada and the United States as to the areas offering the greatest prospects to immigrants; details of his own trips to Canada and the United States and the tickets he used; posters advertising the benefits of North America; lists of subscribers to the various funds he set up; offers of assistance from the Rector of Killarney, G.R. Wynne, who had Canadian connections; information concerning the rates of wages in Canada and the conditions of employment; news as to how those he had helped had fared; pleas for help from those who wished to emigrate; and correspondence regarding Foster's contacts with members of the Canadian government, including Sir John MacDonald and J.H. Pope, regarding their policy on immigration. There are also copies of printed pamphlets. Foster's own publication, *Emigration to North America* contains letters from Canadian Emigration Agents and the pamphlet entitled *Family Emigration from the East of London* provides information on the number of emigrants from that area and their reception in Canada. **D.3618/D/3/2, /6/12, 23, 24, / 7/7, 8, 10, /8/7, 9, /9/8-12, /10/1-3, 7-10, /11/1-3, /15/45, 58, 88, /16/1, /23/12, /24/1, /25/15, / 27/2, /28/1-3**

Five letters, 1863-9, from Edmund Lettson, Haldimand, Canada, and New York and New Orleans, to his parents, Glenavy, Co. Antrim, giving a highly detailed account of his journey from Belfast to Quebec and then by train to Haldimand, where his grandparents lived. He moved on to the United States and his later letters have only passing references to Canada.
D.3673/1, 6-9

Letter, 5 April 1864, from Mary Cummings, Haldimand, Ontario, to Eliza Bolton, [Ireland], concerning family news.
D.3673/2

Records, 1893-1971, of Robinson & Cleaver Ltd, Royal Irish Linen Warehouse and later department store of Belfast, Banbridge, Co. Down, Ballykelly, Co. Londonderry, London and Liverpool, England. They include foreign order registers with orders from Canada.
D.3678/11/1-3

Letter, 30 December 1816, from Samuel Brown, U.S.A., to his nephew, James Brown, Belfast, mentioning a mutual friend, Mr Young, who had been offered 1000 acres of land in Canada by the English Consul in New York.
D.3688/F/9

Letter, 1 February 1820, from Thomas Batt, Belfast, to James Brown, Philadelphia, Pennsylvania, complaining about the influx of cheap Quebec timber.
D.3688/F/19

Handwritten transcript, c.1880, of newspaper report relating to riots following an Orange procession at Harbour Grace, Newfoundland.
D.3692/3

Letter, 19 June 1843, from James Keilty, New York, to William Galbraith, Dundonald, Belfast, commenting on 'Irish meetings for to aid Dan O'Connell'. He said that the speeches were violent and were by the same speakers who figured so largely in the Canadian troubles.
D.3693/E/1

Copy letter, 30 September 1813, from John Lang, 'with the army before Fort George, Niagara', Upper Canada, to Acheson Lyle, Lodge, Co. Londonderry, commenting on the topography of the area and giving details of his regiment's movements since their arrival in Canada.
D.3703/G/1

22 black and white photographs, 1868-70, 23 cm by 18 cm which record Alexander Robb's journeys in British Columbia on the Thomson and Fraser Rivers. They include views of: the two rivers; the gold rush towns of Lytton, Yale, Quesnelle and Barkerville; gold claims and equipment; mule trains; a paddle steamer; coast Indians; Indian salmon drying racks and storage cache; Victoria, Vancouver; the Alexandra suspension bridge; 'Jack Ass' mountain; and wagon roads. (*See also* T.1454).
D.3758/1-22

Papers, compiled 1960-79, of F. McKee, a member of Lisburn Historical Society, Lisburn, Co. Antrim. They consist largely of his historical and genealogical notes relating to the history of Lisburn and its families. There are several passing references to Canada, including a comment on the efforts of Hugh McCall to obtain assisted passages to enable Lisburn people to emigrate to Canada in the 1860s.
D.3771

Business papers, 1935-71, of R. & H. Hall, grain merchants, Belfast, including references to trade with Canada.
D.3798

Souvenir booklet, 1982, of Coleraine Academical Institution's rugby tour to British Columbia.
D.3802

Correspondence, title deeds, mortgages, abstracts of title, leases and other papers, 1798-1950, relating to the Maxwell family's ownership of Amherst Island, Ontario. The island was acquired by the 3rd Earl of Mount Cashell in 1835 and he encouraged and sponsored Irish settlement there. But he was forced to sell to Robert Perceval Maxwell in 1857 and the bulk of this archive deals with this transfer. The Perceval family owned property on the island until the 1950s and other documents reflect this interest with rental lists, valuations and surveys of tenants being included.
D.3817/1/1-2, /2/1-8 and /3/1-16

Correspondence, 3 July-31 December 1958, of the 8th Earl of Antrim whilst he was chairman of the Northern Ireland region of the National Trust. It includes a report on the visit of Robin Fedden to Canada and the United States. Closed to the public until 1994.
D.3839/B/11

13 letters, May 1834-September 1838, from William Lapenstier and his aunt, Mrs Mercy Graves, both of Castledawson, Co. Londonderry, to George Ackworth, solicitor, Rochester, Kent, England, concerning the sale of property at Brompton, Kent. Lapenstier wanted to emigrate to Canada and was trying to raise capital.
D.3861/5/1-13

Log book, 11 March 1740-6 October 1742, of *H.M.S. Furnace*, under the command of Christopher Middleton. The ship was on a voyage seeking a passage through Hudson's Bay to the South Sea. She sailed from Deptford, Kent, and the log has daily entries on weather conditions, the ship's movements at sea and the occupation of the crew at Churchill, Hudson's Bay, where they built a fort and constructed a harbour. The log provides a good description of life in the Sub-Arctic during the period with details of the Indians in the area and the activities of the

Plate 3: Survey party, c.1880.
(PRONI ref. D.552/B/3/5/3)

Plate 4: View of port of Montreal, c.1880.
(PRONI ref. D.552/B/3/5/3)

Hudson's Bay Co. In April 1742 the *Furnace* left Churchill and began an exploratory voyage of the area and details are given of the recording of discoveries and the naming of various features.
T.416/1

Log book, 13 May 1746-30 April 1747, of the *California*, under the command of Francis Smith. This ship was on a similar voyage to that of the *Furnace* and the entries in the log follow the same format.
T.416/2

Transcripts, 1694-1774, of the Dobbs family papers.
T.431

Letter, 31 March 1716, from Henry Maxwell, [?], to [?], Finnebrogue, Co. Down. Finnebrogue was the home of the Perceval-Maxwell family. The Canadian reference is found in Maxwell's suggestion that it was '.... a proper time to send colonies from North Britain to settle in Annapolis Royal and Newfoundland, so that the former at least may hereafter be maintained without the expense of a garrison. ....'.
T.448 p.277

Second report of Mr. Edward Oswald, 8 November 1838, suggesting collaboration with the Canada or British Land Co., to remove tenants from the Merchant Taylors' Irish estate to Canada.
T.656 p.449

Correspondence and reports, June 1727-June 1729, between the British and Irish administrations concerning emigration from the north of Ireland to the British colonies in America which was considered to have reached detrimental levels. The correspondents include the 1st Duke of Newcastle, Primate Boulter, Thomas Wyndham and the 1st Earl Granville.
T.659 pp. 59, 64 and 74-80

Extracts, 1833-5, from Ordnance Survey notes of emigration lists for townlands in Co. Londonderry. They provide information on the name, age, religion, townland of residence and date of departure of the emigrants. The destinations are also given and include St John, New Brunswick and Quebec, as well as various ports in the United States. (*See also* T.768/1).
T.671/1-2

Letter, 3 August 1814, from Adam Duffin, Halifax, Nova Scotia, to his wife, Ellen, Broughshane, Co. Antrim. He refers to his schemes having been foiled by the war between the United States and Britain but he does not elaborate on their nature.
T.710/6

Abbreviated typescript copy of a genealogical sketch of the Dickie family of King's County, compiled in 1909 by the Rev. Henry Dickie, Chatham, Ontario.
T.728/1

List, 1833-4, of emigrants from Coleraine parish, Co. Londonderry, giving information on the names, ages, religion, townlands of residence and date of departure of those involved. The destinations are also given and include St John, New Brunswick, and Quebec.
T.768/1

Legal papers, 1751, used in the law suit Armstrong *v.* Armstrong, which was concerned with the administration of the estate of Lt Col Lawrence Armstrong of Nova Scotia, who died leaving property in Ireland.
T.808/p.536

Copy of extracts, 1838-9, from letters and journals of Robert Peel Dawson, 2nd Grenadier Guards in England, Canada and the United States. Dawson was a member of the British reinforcements sent to deal with the civil unrest in Canada during these years. His papers include an account of the voyage to Quebec, descriptions of tours he made in Canada and the United States during periods of leave and details of his regiment's role in dealing with the 1838 rebellion. Reference is also made to a discussion with Sir John Colborne about the issues of the rebellion.
T.850

Emigration lists, 1802-11, for the port of New York, with references to immigrants from both Ireland and Canada. Details are given of the immigrant's name, the date of arrival and the point of departure.
T.1011/1-4

The papers of interest in this collection concern Canada's involvement in the American War of Independence. John Maxwell of Falkland, Co. Monaghan, served on the staff of Sir Guy Carleton, Governor of Quebec, during the war years. Several of the documents refer to American attempts to win Canadian support and the subsequent Canadian reaction. They include:

Loyal address, September 1774, of the Canadian citizens of Quebec to George III, dissociating themselves from '... murmures du tres petit nombre....';
T.1023/112

Letter, 21 February 1775, from 'Samuel Adams, Wm Mackay, Joseph Warren, on behalf of the Boston Committee of correspondence, to Zachy McCauley, John Aitken, John Lee, John Patterson, John Wells, Randal Meredith, and other friends of liberty in Quebec, arguing the American cause'.;
T.1023/113

Draft of a reply, 12 April 1775, to the above, criticizing the actions of the Continental Congress and suggesting that Canadian opinion was not as the Americans perceived it. Ignorance and the power of the priests were blamed for preventing the 'enlightened men' from having much effect. A speedy relief to their grievances against the Quebec Act was expected from the next Parliament;
T.1023/114

Letter, 18 May 1775, from Ethan Allen, Commander of the American Army at St John, New Brunswick, to James Morrison and the '... merchants that are friendly to the course of liberty in Montreal ...', demanding provisions for the Continental Army;
T.1023/115

'Resolutions of His Majesty's loyal subjects and inhabitants of the city of Quebec', 20 July 1775, to form a company for the defence of property, peace and order in the city;
T.1023/116

Four letters, 22 October-6 December 1775, from the American General, Richard Montgomery, to various correspondents, including Sir Guy Carleton, demanding the surrender of Montreal and Quebec, warning of the consequences if the town's stores were destroyed and complaining of ill-treatment of American prisoners of war;
T.1023/117-120

Letter, 19 January 1776, from Donald Campbell to Colonel Allan McClean, thanking him for General Montgomery's watch and referring to the treatment of prisoners of war;
T.1023/121

Monthly return, 1 April 1776, of H.M. Forces in the garrison at Quebec;
T.1023/122

Letter, 29 April 1776, from General Schuyler, Saratoga, New York, to Colonel Patterson, [?], giving detailed orders for his regiment to go to Quebec;
T.1023/123

Copy letter, 24 May 1776, from Moses Hazen, La Prairie, Quebec, to the Commissioners of Congress at Montreal, describing a visit to Benedict Arnold's camp and discussing policy towards the Indians;
T.1023/124

Printed circular, (in French), 31 January 1778, from H.T. Cramahé, Quebec, to the officers of the militia, asking for continued vigilance and announcing the rates of compensation for those who took part in the campaigns of 1776 and 1777;
T.1023/125

Letter (in French), 18 September 1778, from Jas. Livingston, La Point Olivie, Quebec, to the officers of the militia, requesting them to bring their men to La Point Olivie and conveying the thanks of General 'Bastonay'.
T.1023/126

Letter, 5 July 1837, from James Heather, Montreal, Quebec, to Thomas Greeves, Dungannon, Co. Tyrone, referring to a law suit in which Heather is involved and stating that he is finding life difficult as an emigrant in Canada.
T.1059/1

Letter, 8 January 1808, from Thomas Black, Prince of Wales Islands, to 'My dear uncle', [?]. Black has been in Canada for a year and a half with the 20th Regiment. He describes his duties and the Islands he is on and complains of the high cost of living.
T.1073/49/1-2

Letter, 23 March 1935, from J.A. Ready, Toronto, Ontario, to Mrs Duffin, Belfast, referring to family news and history.
T.1116/53

Three letters, 5 November 1819-5 June 1820, from Robert McClorg, Philadelphia, Pennsylvania, and John McClorg, St John, New Brunswick, to their father, David, Templemoyle, Co. Londonderry. The brothers emigrated together but separated after their arrival in Canada. Robert describes the voyage and the search for work which led him to Philadelphia. He compares the United States to Canada, finding in favour of the latter. He also refers to the fortunes of other Londonderry emigrants and advises his brothers against leaving Ireland, '... for if I could have got situations at home, I would not have come here ....'. John describes his employment with Amos Purley, a member of the House of Assembly of New Brunswick, and complains that the constant arrival of emigrants makes it very difficult to find work.
T.1227/4, 5, 7

Two letters, 3 June and 3 August 1814, from Adam Duffin, London, England, and Halifax, Nova Scotia, to Mrs Ellen Duffin, Broughshane, Co. Antrim, concerning his voyage to South Carolina *via* Halifax during the Anglo-American war.
T.1252/27-28

Three letters and a diary, 1881-1930, of John J. Elder, Ashgrove, Co. Donegal, and Toronto, Ontario. The diary, 1881-98, has daily entries and describes Elder's early Irish life and his emigration to Canada on 15 April 1887. He travelled with his brother, Andrew, and three friends from Moville, Co. Donegal, on board the *S.S. Sardinian*. It also includes chronological lists of marriages and deaths of the Elder family. This appears to be a copy of the original diary and it is endorsed to 'Jeanie M. Tynan, January 12, 1927'. The three letters, 1928-30, are from Elder to his cousin, J.F. Caldwell, Belfast, concerning Elder's genealogical research and giving details of other emigrant families. **T.1264/3a, b, c** and **/6**

Letter, 1890, from J.J. Elder, New Brunswick, to John Caldwell, Belfast, concerning the genealogy of the Caldwell and Porterfield families, Ballymagorry, Co. Tyrone.
T.1320

Two letters, 14 March 1816 and 15 May 1823, from William Bingham, Barnamaghery, Co. Down, to his brother, Andrew, Etobico, Ontario, relating family and political news from Ireland and complaining of the high price of land and the diminished value of agricultural produce following the end of the Napoleonic wars. He gives news of other people from the area who are to emigrate to Canada and asks his brother for information about his life there. Reference is also made to a land dispute in Canada amongst Irish emigrants who have written home for assistance.
T.1332/1-2

Letter, 1849, from Richard Breathwait, Cannington, Ontario, to his parents, Lisburn, Co. Antrim, describing his home area in the township of Brook and its development since the arrival of the first white settlers in 1820. He also describes farming conditions in the area and gives an excellent list of market prices for agricultural commodities. Reference is made to the popularity of Irish newspapers in Canada and to the '... great fun in Montreal in April last ....' following the passage of the Bill of Indemnity which provided compensation for the rebels' losses during the 1838 rebellion.
T.1362/1

Two letters, 1845, from F.R.M. Crozier to his sisters, Banbridge, Co. Down, referring to his appointment as second-in-command to Sir John Franklin on the expedition to discover a North West passage. The second letter, from on board the *Terror* was the last received by his family and refers to the progress made by the expedition in June as they sail for Davis Strait.
T.1424/1-2

Nine letters, 10 August 1862-8 July 1873, from Alexander Robb, Nicola Lake, Lytton, British Columbia, to his family, Dundonald, Co. Down, concerning his fortunes in Canada. The first letter describes his journey from Vancouver to Cariboo to prospect for gold and he gives a vivid account of the hardships faced by prospectors in Cariboo. With his savings absorbed he was forced to move on and his letters from 1868 describe his life as a farmer in British Columbia, first as an employee engaged in opening a stock raising farm and then as a partner in a 320 acre tract. There is a glowing report of the agricultural opportunities in Canada, although he complains of the isolation caused by the lack of roads. He enjoys good relations with the Indians and gives an account of their habits, along with a survey of the way in which white settlement has progressed in the region. There is a discussion of the effects of Dominion status and the prospect of a new railway being constructed. Despite his improving situation he is lonely and homesick and asks his sister to find a wife for him.

20 black and white photographs, 1860s and 70s, which record Alexander Robb's journeys in British Columbia on the Thomson and Fraser Rivers. They include views of; the two rivers; the gold rush towns of Lytton, Yale, Quesnelle and Barkerville; gold claims and equipment; mule trains; paddle steamer; coast Indians; Indian salmon drying racks and storage cache; Rocky Point school house; Nicola Valley; 'Jack Ass' Mountain; wagon roads; and the Alexandra suspension bridge.
T.1454/5/9-16, /6/1 and **/7/1-20**

Ticket, c.1860, issued by J. & J. Cooke's American Passenger Office, Londonderry, for a passage to St John, New Brunswick, aboard *S. V. Elizabeth*.
T.1455

Three documents, 1790-94. Agreement, with transcript, 1790, between the Crown and the Indians relating to the lands on the north side of Lake Erie.
Appointment of Alexander McKee as 'Deputy Superintendant General and Deputy Inspector General of the Indians inhabiting the Provinces of Upper and Lower Canada, 1794'.
T.1473

Notice of sailing, 1847, of the *Lady Caroline* of Newry, from Warrenpoint, Co. Down, to St John, New Brunswick.
T.1498

Letter, 26 July 1843, from Charlotte Bacon, Montreal, Quebec, to her parents, Newtownlimavady, Co. Londonderry, giving news of her progress in Canada and that of other emigrants known to her family. She refers to her intention to pay back the money her grandmother lent her for the voyage and encloses money from another emigrant to his family.
T.1639/5

Letter, 22 May 1888, 'Robb', Toronto, Ontario, to his sister 'Annie', [Ireland], complaining bitterly that Canada is overcrowded with emigrants and blaming the emigration agents for this.
T.1639/7

Letter, 25 April 1827, from John Jennings, Saintfield, Co. Down, to Robert McKee, on board the ship *Bolivar* at Quebec. The letter contains news of old acquaintances and agricultural activity in the Saintfield area.
T.1686

Letter, 26 March 1821, from Robert Wray, Peterscreek, Quebec, to his mother and brothers, Coleraine, Co. Londonderry, describing his meeting with his brother, James, and other friends from Ireland.
T.1727

Three letters, 1929-35, concerning Norman Lewis as an emigrant to Ontario, and all containing family news.
T.1776

Two letters, 5 and 10 December 1893, from C. Hobson, New York, to his niece, Jane, Richhill, Co. Armagh, giving a detailed account of his journey to Ontario to visit friends, his reception there and the manner in which he spent his holiday. He compares labourers' wages and farming methods in Ontario to those in New York and he describes his tour to Niagara Falls. There is also a small sketch of the Falls.
T.1795/1-2

12 letters, 1897-9, from Elizabeth Fleming, Owen Sound, Ontario, to her cousin, [Castlereagh area of Belfast?]. They are almost entirely concerned with the possibility of her acquiring a legacy from the estate of her late aunt, Jane Brown.
T.1850/1-12

Two letters, 14 and 19 April 1847, from J. & J. Cooke, Londonderry, to Rev. Robert Gage, Rathlin Island, concerning the difficulties in accommodating 80-100 passengers on the emigrant ship, the *St John*, bound for Quebec.
T.1883/63, 64

Letter book, 1771-4, dealing with the affairs of the estate of the 5th Earl of Donegall. The problems the land agents faced in administering the estate led to the emigration of tenants and letters written after April 1773 deal with the question of emigration to North America and the implications for the Donegall estate.
T.1893

Pedigree, c.1825-c.1962, of the O'Brien and Archibald families, Londonderry and Nova Scotia.
T.1899/1

Letter, 1890, from Rosetta Watson Kerr, Lachute, Quebec, to an anonymous correspondent containing genealogical notes concerning the Watson family, Lurgan, Co. Armagh, c.1800-1860.
T.1903/2

Newspaper cutting, 1842, referring to advertisements for emigrant ships sailing to New York and Quebec from Ireland.
T.1904/1

Three letters, 14-17 December 1821, between W.A. Clubbey, Secretary to the Governor, Fort Cornwallis, and R. Cannter, Superintendent of Police, Prince of Wales Island, on the one hand, and William Jamieson on the other. They concern the granting of official permission to Jamieson to leave Canada 'and to proceed to Europe in the ship *Amity*'.
T.1956/8-10

Manuscript journal, 'A Pedestrian Tour to the Falls of Niagara in Upper Canada: May 1814-June 1815' by Samuel Holmes, an army surgeon, 81st Regiment of Foot. The journal begins with the voyage from Cork to Quebec, his travels by foot from Quebec to Niagara, where he joins his regiment, his experiences in the Anglo-American war, from General Drummond's withdrawal from Fort Erie to the end of the conflict. In May 1815, he embarks by boat for Quebec, sailing from there to Portsmouth where the journal ends. The journal contains many detailed observations and includes appendices with lists referring to the names and salaries of the officers of the Provincial Parliament of Upper Canada. There is also a list of the prices of provisions during his tour.
T.1970/4/1-116

34 letters, 1876-94, from: John and Ann Walker, Caulfield, Ontario; Martha Cranston, Tapleytown, Ontario; Mary S. Cranston, Tapleytown and Hamilton, Ontario; John A. Walker, North Cayuga, Ontario; Maggie J. Lowry, Caulfield, Ontario; and Anne Jane Knox, Clanbrassil, Ontario. They are all addressed to Andrew Lowry, Ballindrait, Co. Donegal, the uncle of most of these correspondents. They provide extensive information on agricultural prices, conditions and techniques, and on the movements of the various families within Canada. The letters of John Walker, Caulfield, a farm machinery salesman, are of particular interest as he furnishes his uncle with an account of the development and cost of the new agricultural technology. There are also complaints about the cost of entertaining visiting dignitaries such as Lady Stanley in 1888 and some discussion of Canadian politics, in particular the issues surrounding the Jesuit Bill of 1889. One other letter, that of 21 September 1894, from I. Blair, Keelogs, Ballindrait, Co. Donegal, to Andrew Lowry, requests that Lowry writes to Blair's uncle in Canada.
T.2018/4, 6, 7, 8, 11-39, 41

Papers relating to Moses Staunton, paper manufacturer, formerly of Glencairn, Belfast, who sailed for Toronto, Ontario, in 1854. He died 3 October 1877 and was interred at Mount Pleasant, Toronto. His descendants are believed to be leading paper producers in Toronto. The documents include:

Letter, 27 September 1854, from R.J. Staunton, Liverpool, England, to his mother and sister, Glasgow, Scotland, referring to the shipwreck involving Moses Staunton and his family, 70 miles from St John's, Newfoundland. All were saved.
T.2035/11

Letter, 25 September 1856, from Moses Staunton, Toronto, Ontario, to his mother and sister, [Glasgow], describing his establishment as a shopkeeper and paper manufacturer. Information is also given about his other property speculation, the general conditions in the country, wages and family news. He did not advise anyone to emigrate to Canada unless they were prepared to work hard.
T.2035/13

Documents, 1877-9, concerning the death of Moses Staunton and his wife, Rebecca, both in Toronto.
T.2035/17-19

Letter, 1843, from Amy Douglas and her son, Newtownstewart, Co. Tyrone, to her brother, Alexander McGough, Ontario, concerning family news.
T.2076

Letter, 6 May 1793, from James Green, St John, New Brunswick, to Rev. James Irwin, Ireland. Green was a soldier and he vehemently attacked the French for their declaration of war on Britain and hoped that Ireland would remain loyal. He suggests that he may get promotion as many of the officers have left the army to settle in Upper Canada.
T.2093/6

Letter, 28 February 1807, from E.I., Quebec, to his father, Rev. James Irwin, Ireland, concerning family and social news.
T.2093/28

Letter, 28 March 1758, from H. Pringle, Fort Carrillon, to Colonel Haviland, Fort Edward, describing the aftermath of a battle with the French and Indians on the 13th March. The British force had retreated on the arrival of the Indians and Pringle's detachment became separated from their comrades and were lost in the woods. They were ill-prepared for the harsh winter weather and were forced by exhaustion to surrender to the French garrison at Carrillon. The original of this letter is in the Royal Inniskilling Fusiliers' Museum, Omagh, Co. Tyrone.
T.2095

Two letters, February 1850 and 9 May 1852, from Isaac and Abraham Topley, Montreal, Quebec, to their father Abraham, and their brother-in-law, James Boardman, Co. Armagh, describing the general conditions in the country, their travels and giving a list of prices of provisions and transport. Abraham refers to the fortunes of other Irish immigrants he knows and explains his reasons for emigrating and his plans to remarry.
T.2149/1-2

Poster, 1818, advertising the 'First ship for British America', the brig *Industry*, sailing from Warrenpoint, Co. Down, to Port Miramichi, New Brunswick.
T.2151

Genealogical notes, 1766-1964, on the Higgins family, Broomhedge, Magheragall, and Belfast. They were compiled by J.C. Higgins, Ontario, in 1964.
T.2203/2-4

Manuscript, 1952, of typescript lecture notes on Ulster connections with the British Empire by Miss P. Cowan, Secretary of the Ulster Branch of the Overseas League, including lists of Ulster place names used in Canada and of Ulster personalities who have figured in Canadian history. There is also a newspaper extract, [origin unknown], referring to mention in the *Toronto Sentinel* of a citadel of Northern Ireland in Ontario; the town of Baxter. Miss Cowan notes those contacts which she has made in Canada.
T.2207/3

Letter, 9 August 1857, from Robert Francis Byron, Trenton, Canada West, to his brother, Owen, [Ireland], describing his living conditions and offering his assistance to his brother if he wishes to emigrate.
T.2227/2

Letter, 21 March 1819, from John Duff, Drumconvis, Co. Tyrone, to James Duff, tallow chandler, Philadelphia, Pennsylvania, in which he comments that '... all the boys in general about this place are going next week with Jno. Brown to Quebec as intending for Philadelphia as soon as possible .. in all 150 about this place goes together. ....'.
T.2252/2

Photograph, c.1914, of Lieutenant-Colonel J.W. Boyle, Chief of the Canadian Commission to Rumania.
T.2273

Letter, 8 July 1884, from John Gribben, Toronto, Ontario, to William John Thompson, Carrickfergus, Co. Antrim, giving a detailed account of his departure from Ireland and his voyage to Canada on board the *Sardinian*. He also refers to his search for employment on arrival.
T.2278/4

Two letters, 6 and 8 November 1897, from A.S. Woodburn, Ottawa, to 'Cousin Lowry' and Annie H. Mayne, Belfast, giving an account of his life in Canada since leaving Ireland in 1841 and discussing progress made in that time, especially in Ottawa, including the laying of streets and pavements, the spread of electrical power and improvements in the postal service. Reference is also made to the way in which Irish newspapers were distributed amongst immigrant families.
T.2284/1/8-9

Seven weekly articles, 9 January-20 February 1938, from *The Sunday Chronicle* on the life of Lord Craigavon by Sir Wilson Hungerford. They include comment on Craigavon's role as a '..... commercial traveller ...' for Ulster in Canada when he visited Canada as Prime Minister of Northern Ireland in 1926.
T.2291

Letter, 30 October 1903, from John [? Qutle], Saskatoon, Saskatchewan, to Alexander Taylor, [Ireland], concerning his hopes for the development of Saskatoon as the prospect of railroad construction approaches and land prices within the town increase. References are also made to his employment and to his inspection of the local flax crop which he feels is thicker and stronger than Irish flax. He hopes to employ Russian settlers to pull it as their labour appears to be cheapest.
T.2296/7

Letter, 1 January 1827, from David Baily, Boston, Massachusetts, to his brother, John, Donaghedy, Co. Tyrone, about the '... grate many strange places and faces [*sic*] ....' he has seen since leaving Ireland, including some in Canada. He encourages his brothers to join him.
T.2332

Three letters, 14 March 1870-7 January 1874, from 'Emma', Oxley and Colchester, Ontario, to her cousin, 'Nancy', Ballymena, Co. Antrim, concerning family news.
T.2338/4-6

Incomplete letter, c.1900, from John Craig, [Canada] to [?], [Ireland], drawing comparisons between the quality and cost of life in Canada and that found in Ireland, preferring the former.
T.2338/21

Emigrant letters sent to E.R.R. Green, Manchester University, Manchester, as a result of his appeal for letters from Irish emigrants. These are copies of the Staunton letters at T.2035.
T.2345/3-4

Letter, c.1762, from Edward Willes, Chief Baron of the Exchequer whilst on circuit in Ireland, to Sally Wise, England, referring to the extent of emigration from the Coleraine and Londonderry areas to Nova Scotia.
T.2368/4

Letter, 20 July 1819, from Robert Love, Petersburg, Virginia, to John Love, Banbridge, Co. Down, describing a voyage from Belfast to Baltimore. Included is a reference to a sighting of the brig, *Navigator* which was sailing from Jamaica to Quebec with a cargo of rum and sugar. The water cases of the *Navigator* had been eaten through by rats and she was supplied with replacements by the ship on which Love was travelling.
T.2393/2/4A-B

17 annual balance sheets and trading accounts, August 1908-August 1924, of William Dalzell & Sons, shipping agent, The Quay, Coleraine, Co. Londonderry. The company was involved in the emigrant trade to Canada.
T.2403/2-18

Typescript account of the military career of Lieutenant James Prendergast of Co. Monaghan and his settling in Canada, 1789-1834. He enlisted in the 100th Prince Regent's Regiment of Dublin in 1805 and arrived in Canada in September 1805. His contingent became part of the Old Fighting 99th and he saw much action, mostly during the Anglo-American war of 1812-14, including Sackett's Harbour, Black Rock, Chippewa and Plattsburg. He was demobbed in 1818 and returned to Ireland. In 1825 some of his family emigrated to Canada and he followed them shortly afterwards, becoming the Land Agent for Clarendon, Lower Canada, in 1826 and receiving a 500 acre grant for himself. He died of cholera in Quebec city in 1834.
T.2410

Two letters, 14 September and 20 October 1853, from William McElderry, Liverpool, England, and Lynchburg, Virginia, to an anonymous correspondent on board the *Sarah Sands*, referring to his voyage to Quebec and his journey to Lynchburg. He says he would have gone *via* Philadelphia, Pennsylvania, but the ships for that port were full.
T.2414/10-11

Emigrant ship advertisements, late 18th century, taken from the *Belfast News Letter* and including mention of the *Nelson Village* sailing to Quebec.
T.2428/1

Letter, 18 June 1821, from Elizabeth Boardman, Port Hope, Upper Canada, to her father, James Boardman, Tandragee, Co. Armagh, giving details of health, weather and requesting family news.
T.2460/1-2

Two volumes, May 1825-May 1826, entitled 'Remarks on a voyage of discovery to the Pacific and Bhering's [*sic*] Straits on board *H.M.S. Blossom*, compiled by Richard Beechey, then a 15 year old midshipman. The *Blossom* was to rendez-vous with Franklin's second overland expedition and the time spent waiting for the rendez-vous was to be employed '... in making useful observations amongst the islands and other places in the Pacific ...', and these notes give a summary description of the voyage. The first volume describes the Pacific voyage, the second the Arctic one. 387 pages.
T.2479/2-3

Sketch book, 1825-6, entitled 'Views of Pacific etc., islands/book drawn by R. Beechey MIDn/ aged 14 *H.M.S. Blossom*'. The reproductions are black and white photographs with the size of the originals not being evident from them. There are 69 marine topographical views, although portions of some of them are missing. A few of the sketches are in pencil, the rest watercolour. Many of the sketches are of the Pacific, but about 12 are of Alaska or the Bering Strait, with the names given not being modern. These show ships, birds and kayaks in the distance. There are also views of the coast north from California, including a view of what might be a canoe of west coast Indians, depicting weapons, hats and blankets. It is entitled 'St Lawrence Islands'. 44 pages complete with negative copy.
T.2479/4-5

Six letters, 15 January 1863-10 November 1869, from James D. Collins, Peterborough, Ontario, to relatives and friends, Falmore, Co. Donegal. He describes how he fared since his arrival in Canada from Ireland, having worked in the grain business before setting up on his own. He requests that two young men be sent out who will help him to farm and he offers his assistance to them. There is also an account of a deer hunting expedition.
T.2487/1/51, 52, 54, 55, 58, 60

Letter, 23 August 1883, from Latimer Whittle, Peter's Rock, Kingston, Ontario, to 'My dearest Maria', [?] requesting money to prevent his property being confiscated.
T.2487/1/66

Letter, c.1850, anonymous, off the Banks of Newfoundland, to 'My dears', [?], giving an account of the voyage from Ireland, which has been good.
T.2487/1/125

Newspaper cutting, undated, from an unidentified Canadian newspaper describing the discovery in Ballynahinch, Co. Down, of various promissory notes in a secret drawer in a rosewood deed box.
T.2489/7A-B

Shipping agent's account book, 1855-9, of William McCorkell & Co., Londonderry, giving details of cargoes carried, insurance rates paid, dock duties and some passenger lists. There are statements for voyages to St John, New Brunswick, and Quebec but most of the business is in the United States and the Caribbean.
T.2511/3

Typescript diary, 1832-1917, of David McCloy, Ballymena, Co. Antrim, and Preston, Ontario. Following the arrival of favourable reports from relatives who had settled in the Huron district, Alexander McCloy, David's father, took his family to Canada in 1847. This diary gives an account of their voyage and settlement, with detailed descriptions of David's own experiences. He acquired a farm near Berlin (now Kitchener), Ontario, in 1857 and became an influential member of the local community, helping to establish a school at Mornington, Ontario, and taking a seat in the town council. He died in 1917. The diary also refers to the activities of his brothers

and sisters and of his own offspring. The appendix provides notes on the genealogy of Annie Byren's family, David's wife.
T.2515

Photocopy of part of a printed short autobiography, 1930, entitled *The travels and philosophy and life and times of Daniel Mooney*, 'an Irish exile, born 1860, on the road between Banbridge and Dromore, Co. Down', and printed in Winnipeg, Manitoba. This photocopy was supplied by the Metropolitan Toronto Library Board.
T.2551/9

Three letters, 8 February 1882-8 January 1883, from G. McKean, St John, New Brunswick, and Brooklyn, New York, to his brother, Edward McKean, Shanghai, China, about the financial difficulties he was facing with his business partner, Francis Carvill. The business eventually collapsed but McKean claimed to own 20,000 acres of timber in Nova Scotia, which he sold for a profit of $42,000. He also comments on the opportunities for speculation in the North-West Territories with the construction of the Canadian Pacific Railroad.
T.2581/67

Pamphlet and programme, 1966, of the unveiling of a historical plaque commemorating 'The Typhus Epidemic, 1847', Kingston, Ontario.
T.2599/3

Two letters, 19 April 1960 and 28 February 1973, of Professor Hereward Senior, McGill University, Montreal, Quebec, concerning books on Irish history.
T.2602/7-8

Letter, 2 August [1834], from Mrs C. Scott, Kingston, Upper Canada, to Mrs Maria Scott, Clifton, Bristol, England, mainly concerning her sister's courtship and engagement with a young clergyman who was employed in missionary work with the Mohawk Indians in the Bay of Quinte. A detailed description is given of his circumstances and living conditions.
T.2609/5

Two letters, 8-14 October 1835 and 8-20 September 1838, from Mrs J. Scott, on board the *Orpheus* and at Picton, Bay of Quinte, to Mrs Anne Scott, Willsborough, Co. Londonderry. The first letter gives an account of the voyage from Ireland to New York with a reference to Newfoundland. The second describes her locality as peaceful but comments on the preparations which were being made for the expected hostilities, including the arrival of the 71st and 83rd Regiments. She is critical of the British Government's 'leniency' and supportive of the Conservative party's criticism of British policy.
T.2609/8, 11

An anonymous account, July 1868, of a voyage from Warrenpoint, Co. Down, to New York, *via* Liverpool, on board the *City of Cork*.
T.2620

Seven letters, 16 June 1819-26 June 1825, from John McBride, Quebec, New Jersey and New York, to his father and brother, Derriaghy, Belfast. The first letter, from Quebec, describes the voyage and the other passengers on board the ship. He felt that it would have been better to have sailed directly to New York, which was his ultimate destination. He moved on to the United States with 24 other immigrants and his letters from there, whilst dealing largely with life in New Jersey and New York, also continue to refer to Canada. He gives news of the fortunes of other Irish immigrants in various parts of Canada, including Quebec and Nova Scotia. He also mentions the celebrations in Kingston, Ontario, following the end of the Queen's trial in 1821.
T.2613/1-3, 5, 8, 10, 12

Pedigree, compiled in 1964 by Desmond B. Rothwell detailing the ancestors and relatives of Desmond and Brian Rothwell, both of whom were living in Montreal, Quebec, in 1961.
T.2621/1/1

Letter, 26 December 1854, from Richard Rothwell, Boston, Massachusetts, to his wife Rosa, Greenisland, Co. Antrim, commenting on a recent, brief trip he made to Canada.
T.2621/2/53

Seven letters, 29 December 1863-12 December 1864, from Richard Rothwell (the son of Richard above), in Canada and the United States, to his mother, Rosa, Ireland. Born in 1845, he emigrated to Canada in 1863 where he worked for the Old Trunk Railroads before returning to Belfast to study engineering at Queen's University. He eventually settled in Australia. These letters refer to his employment in Pointe St Charles, Quebec, his lodgings and his leisure activities, including his work as a Sunday school teacher. There is also a description of his departure from Montreal, Quebec, for New York in 1864.
T.2621/3/1-7

Copy of a book, 1860-68, showing imports of timber by Downpatrick Timber, Slate and Coal Co., Ltd, Church St, Downpatrick, Co. Down. The quantities and sizes of the various types of timber which were imported are given and include some cargoes from: Providentia, Ontario; St John, New Brunswick; and Quebec. The prices, both cost and retail, are given in some cases and comments are made as to the quality of the timber.
T.2623/1

Reminiscences by Bernard Tedford, Old Homestead, New Glasgow, Nova Scotia, of his early days around the Stormont Castle estate, c.1900, and in the Ballyhackamore and Ballymacarret areas of Belfast, c.1870, together with a description of his experiences in Connemara, Galway, c.1880-1890. These papers have less to do with his life in Canada than with his time in Ireland before emigrating but there are some scattered references of interest, including an acknowledgement that he had employed people in his shop in Canada because they had originated from the same part of Ireland as himself. He gives details of the activities of his own offspring and a description of wrestling matches which he has attended in Canada.
T.2629/4/A-B, 2-3

Typescript genealogical notes, c.1650-c.1965, entitled 'These are the McCreights'. Details are given of the McCreight families in Belfast, several townlands in Co. Down, and of those who settled in the United States and in Canada. c.100 pp.
T.2648/3

Letter, 20 November 1848, unsigned, Huntington, Canada West, to his cousin, Joseph Brown, c/o Rev. G.H. Shanks, Saintfield, Co. Down. Having moved on from his original place of settlement, he rented a farm which he hoped to buy. Details are given of the lease and of his work. All of his children were employed and he relates their terms of employment and their rates of pay along with lists of local prices.
T.2675/1

Letter, 15 May 1873, from [S. Meek], Smith's Falls, Ontario, to 'My dear friend', [Ireland], concerning family news and his involvement in the temperance movement.
T.2675/7

Letter, 6 February 187[1], from Edward Parks, St Sylvestre, Quebec, to his brother, Ireland, concerning their agricultural activities and to their supplementary income derived from weaving. His eldest son has purchased a farm and a description is given of this property. Mention is also

made of the activities of other members of his family and of church life in their community. There is a comment on the effect the European war is having on prices in Canada.
T.2680/2/15

Letter, 2 August 1770, from John Patterson, Galdenach, Co. Donegal, to his cousin, James Cochran, Halifax, Nova Scotia, asking for information of Cochran's activities and of Canada, and commenting on the difficult economic conditions in Ireland.
T.2692

Two letters, 27 December 1867-[?], from Matthew Brooks, Philadelphia, Pennsylvania, to his sister, Rebecca, Ireland, referring to the fortunes of Irish immigrants to Canada who are known to them.
T.2700/5, 7

Diary, 3 November 1888-January 1889, of H.J. Clark's trip to the United States and Canada to promote sales for the firm of William Clark & Sons, linen manufacturers, Upperlands, Co. Londonderry. The document is very faded and badly damaged. There is also a typescript copy which includes a resumé of the trip written by Clark when he was compiling a history of the firm, c.1935.
T.2709/3-4

Copy out-letter book, 1826-34, of William McCorkell & Co., shipping agent, Londonderry. This is a copy of D.2892/2/2.
T.2713/1/A/1

Copy out-letter book, 1837-47, of John Cooke, shipping agent, Londonderry. This is a copy of D.2892/2/1.
T.2713/2/A/1

Passenger books, 1850-71, of J. & J. Cooke, shipping agent, Londonderry. These are typescripts of D.2892/1/2-4.
T.2713/2/B

Photographs, c.1840-c.1860, of ships, bills of sale for ships etc., of J. & J. Cooke, shipping agent, Londonderry.
T.2713/2/C/1

Pedigree, c.1670-c.1950, of the Crawford family, Crawfordsburn, Co. Down. It was compiled by Hugh Crawford in 1950 and includes the Canadian branch of the family. The only Canadian address given is Vancouver, British Columbia.
T.2715/1

Letter, 11 January 1911, from Martha [H.], Winnipeg, Manitoba, to her friend, Lizzie [Throne], [Ireland] describing working conditions and pay in Winnipeg.
T.2722/22

13 letters, 6 December 1912-1 August 1932, from Annie Galbraith of: White House and Ebor, Manitoba; Scarborough, Birchcliffe, Bluffs and Toronto, Ontario; and Sceptre, Saskatchewan, to friends and relatives in Ireland. These letters give an account of her family's movements throughout Canada and of the living conditions experienced in the various places. Information is given of their social as well as working activities and in 1914 she expressed concern as to what Home Rule in Ireland might mean for her relatives there and suggesting that if it took place they should come to Canada.
T.2722/26-38

Letter, 1 November 1932, from Mrs H. Galbraith, Toronto, Ontario, to Miss E. Throne, [Ireland], giving a detailed account of Annie Galbraith's illness and death. Some of her belongings have been sent to Co. Tyrone.
T.2722/39

Two letters, 5 December 1937-5 September 1943, from Martha Kincaid, Winnipeg, Manitoba, to Elizabeth [Throne], [Ireland], giving family news and commenting on the good harvest but complaining of the shortness of the season.
T.2722/41-42

Letter, 20 September 1945, from S.S. Gordon, St Catherine St, Vancouver, British Columbia, to 'Bessie and Withe', [Ireland], referring to the death of a Mr Moore and describing his life and family in Canada. He worked for a large department store.
T.2722/43

Two letters and a memorandum, 6 May 1774-c.1790, of Charles O'Hara. The memorandum concerns the formulation of the Navigation Acts. The letters, both from William Burke, comment on the House of Commons' deliberations on the '... framing of a constitution for Canada ...' in 1774 and later on the capture of St John, New Brunswick, in 1775 by the United States, with details of the numbers of troops involved and the prisoners taken.
T.2812/16/8 and **/25/22, 28**

Part of a printed autobiography of John Macoun, Canadian explorer and naturalist, 1831-1920, published by the Ottawa Field Naturalists Club in 1922. There is an introduction by Ernest Thompson Seton. Macoun was the Assistant Director and Naturalist to the Geological Survey of Canada. This part of the autobiography deals with his family background, with genealogical tables and newspaper notices of his birth and death also included.
T.2834/2/2

Sales book, 1919-53, of William Clark & Sons Ltd, linen manufacturer, Upperlands, Co. Londonderry, with some references to trade with Canada.
T.2835/4

Two letters, 24 June 1824-30 May 1827, from Mrs Elizabeth McMullin, Gananoque, Upper Canada, to her daughters, Newtownlimavady, Co. Londonderry, commenting that the country is much improved and giving examples in the progress of transport and schooling facilities. She advises her daughters to emigrate and gives news of the success of missionaries amongst the Indians with 350 of the Mississagua tribe having been converted. Mention is also made of the agitation caused by the Alien Bill.
T.2858/1/18-19

Letter, 11 November 1848, from Richard Dill, Victoria, British Columbia, to his father, Limavady, Co. Londonderry, stating that he is about to sail for Shanghai and referring to the activities of the London Missionary Society.
T.2858/20

Two letters, c.1925, from Mrs Richard Beale, Sutherlands, Saskatoon, Saskatchewan, to Captain Dominick Heyland, Garvagh, Co. Londonderry, concerning family news.
T.2897/10-11

19 letters, 7 January 1757-16 October 1759, of the 4th Duke of Bedford and concerning the administration of the war in North America and its effects on Ireland. His correspondents include the 4th Duke of Devonshire, Richard Rigby, William Pitt, the 20th Earl of Kildare and

Primate Stone. There are also copies of two letters from General James Wolfe, Halifax, Nova Scotia, to Lord George Sackville, London. These describe his voyage to Halifax and the disposition of the troops there. He commented on his tactics and refers to the misconception about the situation in England. The second letter discusses the actions at Louisbourg and complains about the state of the troops.
T.2915/1/7, 11, 12, 18, 19, 21, 24, 27, 34, /2/2, 29, 31, 49, /4/43, /5/24, 42, 44 and **/8/30**

Correspondence, genealogical notes and photograph, 1862-80, relating to Samuel Bruce and his family. The genealogical notes cover the period, 1775-1880, and contain details of the Bruce family of Belfast. The photograph of Samuel Bruce, '... in his war paint ...' was taken in Belfast. There are also seven letters, 23 June 1862-9 July 1863, from Samuel Bruce, Canada, to his brother, James, [Ireland], concerning two hunting and fishing expeditions on the River Mingan, Quebec. They include references to the difficulty he experienced in obtaining Indian porters and the settlement of a dispute between his party and a group of Indians who were netting fish on the river. Bruce also gives a detailed report of his adventures during the Sioux rising of 1862. Caught up in the fighting on his way to hunt bears, he was besieged by the Sioux at Georgetown and after the evacuation of this town his party was captured by the Chippewas. All of this is colourfully described after his escape to Fort Garry, Red River, Manitoba. Before returning to the east he went on a short buffalo hunting trip, on which he met a group of friendly Indians who helped him find the buffalo. A later letter, written from Peterborough, Ontario, requests his brother to send him his masonic costume.
T.2919/29-32, 34, 37, 38 and **/2/6, 9**

Anonymous letter, 17 January 1863, to the editor of the *Peterborough Review*, Ontario, commenting on the origin and the smoking of Kinnikinic and referring to the experiences of a friend, [possibly Samuel Bruce], among the Indians. This friend is described as having been far travelled and very knowledgable about the Indians of the Dakota territory and in possession of a large number of Indian photographic portraits.
T.2919/1/33

Letter, 13 December 1863, from S.C. Keir, Ottawa, to his sister, Marion Workman, M. Planté, Pau Bassés, Pyrenees, France, giving family news.
T.2921/6/21

Letter, c.1867, from Marion Workman, Montreal, Quebec, to her mother, Marion Workman, Belfast, describing her journey from New York to Montreal.
T.2921/6/51

Letter, 8 April 1848, from Mary Duggan, Kingston, Ontario, to her sister in Dungiven, Co. Londonderry, sending £4 which she says will be enough to pay for her sister's passage to America and giving precise details of the expenses which will be met with *en route*. She is working for John A. MacDonald, M.P. for Kingston, Ontario, at this time, and she says that Canada is a good country for those who are willing to work hard.
T.2946/1

Diary, correspondence and report, 1768-76, relating to the Rt Hon. General John Pomeroy. The diary, September 1768, covers Pomeroy's voyage with the 64th Regiment of Foot to North America. Only the actual sea crossing is recorded. By 1770 he was back in Ireland and the letters and report he received there refer to the activities of the British Army in North America, 1770-76, especially those of his own regiment. In 1775 and 1776 he received letters from J. Stuart and from his nephew, Arthur James Pomeroy, Quebec, describing the Army's movements during the American War of Independence. They include an account of the battle of Bunker Hill and references to the attempts to recruit from the Canadian and Indian population.

Comment is also made on Sir Guy Carleton's preparation of the defences of St John, New Brunswick. Other correspondents include Henry Watson Powell and Lieutenant-Colonel Alexander Leslie, both writing from Halifax, Nova Scotia.
T.2954/5/3, 10-12, 20, 22

Ten letters, 5 May 1882-23 July 1895, from Professor Goldwin Smith of Oxford and Buxton, England and Toronto, Ontario, to Edward Gibson, 1st Baron Ashbourne. Most of the letters deal with British and Irish politics but several of the letters contain Smith's reflections on the Irish across the Atlantic. These are generally of an anti-Irish Catholic nature as he feels that '... the Irish make the worst of Canadian citizens and the best of England's enemies ...' and he suggests that it will be '... some time before the Southern Irishman prospers here [Canada] as a farmer ....'. [*See also* MIC.264].
T.2955/B138/1-10

Copy, 5 October 1878, of a 'Draft of Letters Patent passed under the Great Seal of the United Kingdom, constituting the Office of Governor-General of the Dominion of Canada'.
T.2955/C8/9

Copy, 30 July 1898, of a 'Commission passed under the Royal Sign Manual and Signet appointing the Right Honourable, the Earl of Minto to be the Governor-General of the Dominion of Canada.'.
T.2955/C8/10

The originals of these papers are still in the hands of the owner, G.H. Boyle, Bisbrooke Hall, Uppingham, Rutland, Leicestershire. PRONI has made copies of some of them and calendared the others. None of the papers of Canadian relevance have been copied. They include:

Letters, August-October 1833, from Richard Lewis Gordon, to his father and brother in Ireland. Gordon was a naval officer on the schooner *Monkey* and during these months he was writing from Halifax, Nova Scotia.
T.2966/L/12

Three volumes of a ship's log and seaman's diary, 29 April 1830-1839, kept by Midshipman, subsequently Lieutenant, William E.A. Gordon, and mainly relating to *H.M.S. Blanche* on which Gordon served from 1830-35. The *Blanche* visited Halifax during this period.
T.2966/L/14

Letters, 1834-74, from Thomas Smith Kennedy to his sister in Ireland. The early letters were sent from Guelph, Ontario, to which Kennedy had emigrated.
T.2966/Q/7

Copy of a resolution, 26 April 1893, passed by the Orangemen of Toronto, Ontario, and addressed to Colonel E.J. Saunderson in his capacity as Grand Master of Scotland, protesting against Gladstone's second Home Rule bill.
T.2996/5

Letter, 17 September 1832, from Sampson Brady, Montreal, Quebec, to Miss Fanny Reford, Graystone, Co. Antrim, referring to a cholera epidemic in Quebec and family news. He is finding it difficult to get established in Canada and he feels that Ireland was as good as Canada. He hopes to move on to the United States.
T.3028/32

Two letters, 9 June 1833-9 April 1863, from James A. Reford, Massachusetts and New Jersey, to his family, Graystone, Co. Antrim, concerning his voyage to the United States *via* Quebec and

the short time he spent working in Canada. The second letter gives some details of a shipwreck on the rocks off Halifax, Nova Scotia. There is a much larger body of Reford correspondence but most of it deals with J.A. Reford's time in the United States.
T.3028/B3 and **B9a**

Correspondence, newspaper cutting and genealogical papers, 1948-71, relating to the Reford family of Antrim, and Canada. The letters, from Robert Wilson Reford, Montreal, Quebec and Michael Reford, Aylmer, East Quebec, exchange information on family history with members of the family in Antrim. The genealogical notes cover the period 1632-1971 and a newspaper cutting, 1960, refers to Robert Reford, formerly of Moylinny, Co. Antrim, who emigrated to Canada when he was 14 years old. In later life he was to become a shipping magnate and the governor of McGill University and of the Montreal General Hospital.
T.3029/24, 26, 27, 28A, B, C

Letter, 14 June 1820, from Henry Coulter, St Stephen's, New Brunswick, to the Rev. William Moreland, Portaferry, Co. Down, commenting on the North American economy and the prospects awaiting emigrants. Reference is made to the formation of provincial, county and parochial farming societies and government finance for the sponsoring of new farmers. He notes that the Presbyterian church is organising zealously in New Brunswick and there is some rivalry with the Anglicans. Missionary work is being carried out amongst the '... honest but misrepresented Indians ... .
T.3032/1/1

Part of a journal, 23 July-6 August 1857, kept by G.W. Egan, M.D. during his visit to the United States and Canada. This portion deals only with the period he spent in the neighbourhood of the Niagara Falls and includes a highly detailed description of the Falls and their surrounding area. A copy of an engraving and a poem about the Falls are also included.
T.3056/1/1

21 letters, 11 July 1867-30 May 1869, from Captain Kenneth Howard, later Howard Bury, Toronto, Ontario, and Montreal, Quebec, to his father and sister in Ireland, describing the professional and social life of an artillery officer whilst stationed with the Royal Artillery in Canada. His working duties included attendance at the salute to the first Governor-General of Ontario under the new Dominion legislation and employment in the strengthening of the fortifications at Quebec. Shooting and fishing were the principal sporting activities augmented by excursions to the United States and Niagara Falls and participation in an endless whirl of balls and dinners, including dining with Jefferson Davis. Some comments are made about relations between the soldiers and the civilians with there being little ill-feeling except in Quebec. Mention is also made of an expected Fenian invasion from the United States and the precautions which were being taken to avert it. Howard's ship was wrecked on the way home and they were forced to return to Montreal, a city which he did not like. The Canadian letters are only part of a much wider archive which covers Howard's entire military career.
T.3069/2-3, 54-68, 70-73

A bound volume of typescript copies of emigrant letters, 26 May 1848-7 February 1888, of the McConnell family, Co. Antrim, and Canada. Transcribed by Edwin Seaborn, they were published in *Ontario History*, 1948, Vol XI. The central figure in these letters is Jane McConnell and the early letters concern her relationship with her first husband, Henry Johnson. Johnson left Ireland for Canada after being imprisoned for debt and his letters to his wife describe his voyage to New York and his experience looking for work in Canada West. His account of the social and working conditions in southern Ontario is particularly vivid and detailed. Following her husband's urgent plea to join him in Canada, Jane left Ireland with their two children in 1849, but Henry died of cholera in Montreal, Quebec, before they could be reunited. She remained in

Canada and in 1850 married William Nettleton. Western Ontario was her home until her death in 1885 and she continued to correspond with her family in Ireland and with her sister Isabella who had settled near London, Ontario. An obituary list, a copy of the inscription on the McConnell monument at Muckamore, Co. Antrim, and a family tree are all appended to the letters. The originals are held at the University of West Ontario. Further transcriptions of these letters can be found at T.2319 and T.3478.
T.3081

Letter, undated, from Mary Price, [nee McMullan], Eastons Corner, Wolford, Ontario, to her 'Aunt Elizabeth', Ireland, concerning family news and imploring her to come to Canada and live with her. A description is also given of the practice of acquiring sugar by tapping trees.
T.3102/1/8

Letter, 15 December 1813, from Henry McKibben, naval surgeon, Halifax, Nova Scotia, to his aunt, Miss Ellen McKibben, Portaferry, Co. Down, about his experiences in the 1812 Anglo-American war. He was captured by the Americans and held as a prisoner-of-war at Providence, Rhode Island, for two months.
T.3103/1

Typescript copy of a letter, 25 July 1843, from Mrs Sarah Downey, Ballagh, Co. Fermanagh, to her son and other family members, Crookstown, Ontario, discussing family news, commenting on the [campaign for] repeal of the Union and quoting current market prices.
T.3114/1

Letter, 18 June 1884, from [Thomas] McCullough, on board the ship *Otago*, to Robert [Kennedy], [Ireland], concerning his adventures whilst working on the ship and reminiscing about old times. The ship had been bound for Quebec to pick up a cargo of timber when it ran into trouble and had to be towed to Prince Edward Island.
T.3152/3

Letter, 6 May 1912, from Hugh Kennedy, Toronto, Ontario, to his mother, Belfast, describing his voyage from Belfast to Quebec city. Most of the other passengers on board were Scottish. He gives his first impressions of the country and people as he moved on from Quebec to Toronto and began seeking accommodation and work.
T.3152/6

Papers relating to A.C. Buchanan, Chief Agent for Emigration at Quebec.

Extracts of letters, 1 May 1847, received by Buchanan at Quebec. They were written by the emigration agents at Limerick, Sligo and Londonderry and they comment upon the prospective volume and condition of Irish emigrants to Canada in the coming season.

Passenger list, 11 May 1847, issued by Buchanan giving the date of sailing, the names of the ships involved, their point of departure and the number of passengers carried.

27 page report, 27 December 1847, issued by the Medical Superintendent, Dr Douglas, Quebec, concerning '... the number of emigrants who have been admitted, discharged and who have died at the Grosse Isle quarantine hospital establishment, for the season ending November 3rd ....'. Comparisons are made between that year and previous seasons and there is a discussion of the factors which have led to the great increase in the number of immigrants received at the station, particularly from Ireland. Douglas states that there were twice as many ships and passengers as in previous years and many of these people were diseased, with Grosse Isle being unable to cope with the problems. A detailed statement is provided of the station's operations, including staff

reports and the preparation of accommodation. Lists are given of the ships which arrived at Grosse Isle, complete with information about their departure points and dates, arrival dates, the number of passengers carried and those who died at sea. The manner in which these people were dealt with on arrival is fully documented and the number of those who died subsequently is also noted. Douglas believes that it was the living conditions in Ireland before departure which led to so much disease and he suggests measures which might be taken to prevent a recurrence of the problems in subseqent years. (National Archives of Canada ref. MG.24 B1 vol.22).
T.3168

Letter, 3 January 1876, from William Trimble, Enniskillen, Co. Fermanagh, to his son, John Nevin Trimble, Canada, berating his son's shameful character and giving news from Ireland.
T.3214/26

Three letters, 17 November 1883-[?], involving Sinclair Trimble, Canada. The first two were sent to him by his brother, William Copeland Trimble, whilst the third was sent by Sinclair to Patricia Lally. All three concern Sinclair's poor relations with his family which were preventing him from returning home to take up a job on the staff of his family's Co. Fermanagh newspaper, *The Impartial Reporter.*
T.3214/28, 29, 37

A complete set of issues, 12 September 1833-4 September 1834, of the *Londonderry Shipping List and General Price Current*, published weekly by John Evans of the Custom House. They detail the ships which arrived and departed from Londonderry port, including those coming from or going to Canada. The information provided includes the names of the owners and the ships and details of the cargoes carried.
T.3218

Diary, 1848-91, of William McKinney, of Sentry Hill, Carnmoney, Co. Antrim, the United States, and Canada. On 20 March 1860 he paid his fare from Queenstown, Cork, to New York and from this until his return to Ireland in May 1861 the diary contains short, almost daily entries relating to his time in the United States and Canada. There is an account of the voyage with comments upon the ship's conditions and the other passengers. Many of these contain anti-Catholic remarks. He describes his stay in New York and the journey on to Ottawa where he worked first as a farm labourer and then as a store clerk. There is a great deal of information on the life of the local community and the role he played, particularly in church life as a Sunday school teacher. McKinney also mentions a visit by the Prince of Wales and his laying of a foundation stone at Parliament Buildings. The journey home, the cost and the places visited are all described. The section relating to Canada forms only a small part of the complete 32 volumes of William McKinney's diaries.
T.3234/1 pp. 102/127

Two typescript letters, 25 March 1832 and 8 June 1834, from Robert Chesney, Largy, Portglenone, Co. Antrim, to his daughter and son-in-law, Jane and David McClure, Toronto, Ontario, concerning family news.
T.3238/1-2

Correspondence and reminiscences, 1876-c.1928, of Mary G. Anderson, including references to her emigration to the United States *via* Canada in 1884. Two letters, 28 August and 8 September 1884, from Mrs. Anderson to her mother and father, Wicklow, concern her journey. The first, written on board the *S.S. Peruvian*, describes the voyage to Quebec, and the second comments on her illness and that of the children following their journey from Quebec to Chicago, Illinois. They moved on from here to settle in Whicita, Kansas, and her reminiscences provide more detail on their fortunes. The passage was paid for by the Canadian Government as her husband

had befriended officials of that Government when he worked for the Bank of Ireland in Dublin. He had previously gone to Canada at their expense to view the country and on his return he gave lectures for the benefit of prospective settlers, but decided against settling there himself as he did not think it would suit his wife.
T.3258/4/1-3

Testimonial and letter, 19 April 1851 and 24 May 1868, concerning James Russell, Co. Donegal, and Canada. The testimonial was written by James Carson, Londonderry, and comments on the character of Russell who was emigrating to Ontario. Russell received a letter whilst in Ontario, 24 May 1868, from his sister, Sarah Montgomery, Whitehouse, Co. Antrim, requesting family news and giving a list of provision prices in Ireland. Reference is also made to Irish political events.
T.3281/1-2

Four letters, 9 June 1879-24 April 1889, from family and friends in Co. Donegal to Ann and Robert Russell, Dundalk, Ontario, relating family news.
T.3281/3A-B and /4A-B, 5, 6

Two volume biography, compiled post-1911, and entitled 'Short History of the Experience at Sea of Philip John Heath, born 1853 in Dartmouth, Devon, who spent 45 years as a merchant seaman, 1866-1911'. 184 pages long it includes references to several voyages to Canada.
T.3296

Two letters, 22 May 1874, from the 1st Marquess of Dufferin, Governor General, Government House, Ottawa, to Benjamin Disraeli, British Prime Minister, London, concerning the visit to England of Mr Cartwright, the Canadian Minister of Finance. A letter of introduction is included.
T.3310/2-3

Letter, 3 July 1874, from Sam Moore, master of the barque *Two Fannies*, to Mrs Margaret McDermott, Ireland, informing her of the death of her son, John, in a shipping accident at Sault Ste Marie, Ontario.
T.3311

11 letters, 1875-February 1883, from John Moon, Ottawa, and Winnipeg, Manitoba, to his family and friends in Ireland concerning his prospects of getting a job on his arrival in Ottawa, the conditions there and in Winnipeg, where he moved to in 1881. He bought some land there with the intention of building and he gives details of local prices. He also encloses money for his father.
T.3355/1-11

Four sales ledgers, 1893-1951, of D. Dorman & Co., ships' brokers, insurance agents and general commission agents, Belfast. These contain details of transactions with Canadian companies and with companies which traded with Canada.
T.3409/1-4

A list of Irish people who departed from Bordeaux, France, in the 18th century. It was compiled by Paul Butel of the University of Bordeaux in 1975 and includes one reference to a John Donohue who departed for Quebec in 1759, aged 25.
T.3421

Three letters, 5 July 1846-31 March 1868, from Richard Stewart, Coalisland, Co. Tyrone, and William Stewart, Hull, Yorkshire, to their son and brother respectively, Samuel Stewart, To-

TABLES of Roads, from QUEBEC to ALBANY, and from ALBANY to WILLS'S-CREEK.

Quebec to Albany:

	Quebec	Montreal	F. Frontenac	Oswego	Ox Niagara Falls	F. Datroit
Montreal	170					
F. Frontenac	190	360				
Oswego	80	270	440			
Ox Niagara Falls	200	280	470	640		
F. Datroit	270	470	550	740	910	
ALBANY	695	425	225	305	270	440

Albany to Wills's Creek:

	Albany	Boston	New-Port	New-Haven	New-York	Prince-Town	Philadelphia	Lancaster	New-Castle	Annapolis	Alexandria	Williamsbourg
Boston	150											
New-Port	70	170										
New-Haven	110	170	120									
New-York	89	199	259	146								
Prince-Town	54	143	253	313	186							
Philadelphia	43	97	186	296	356	229						
Lancaster	66	109	163	252	362	442	295					
New-Castle	55	35	78	132	221	331	391	264				
Annapolis	107	114	142	185	239	328	438	498	371			
Alexandria	36	133	120	168	211	265	354	404	524	397		
Williamsbourg	168	171	268	186	303	346	400	489	599	659	532	
Wills's Creek	252	146	163	215	175	241	284	338	427	537	597	470

The following List of British Subjects, in North-America, is taken from the London Magazine, for May 1755, inserted there from exact Militia Roles, &c.

Halifax and Lunenburgh in Nova-Scotia,	5000
New-Hampshire - - -	30,000
Massachusets-Bay - - -	220,000
Rhode-Island and Providence -	35,000
Connecticut - - -	100,000
New-York - - -	100,000
The Jerseys - - -	60,000
Pennsylvania - - -	250,000
Maryland - - -	85,000
Virginia - - -	85,000
North-Carolina - - -	45,000
South-Carolina - - -	30,000
Georgia - - -	6000
The total Number,	1,051,000

French, in America, exclusive of Regulars.
Louisiana 7000
Canada, 45,000. Total, 52,000.

LIST of the Inhabitants in the City and County of N. York, taken in June, 1756.

Males, young and old, - - -	4742
Females under 16, - - -	2359
Females above 16, and under 60, -	3667
Total, Whites,	10,768
Negroes, in the City and County of New-York.	2272

Plate 5: New York Pocket Almanac, 1759. *(PRONI ref. D.679)*

ARE YOU THINKING OF GOING TO CANADA?

ASSURED EMPLOYMENT WITH ASSISTED PASSAGES

FARM WORKERS
With or without experience

FAMILIES SETTLED ON FARMS
With Free Passages for children under 17 years and Loans for Live Stock and Equipment.

— DOMESTIC SERVANTS —

FREE PASSAGES FOR BOYS
between 14 and 17 years

MARRIED COUPLES
With Farming Experience

For further information call and see
Mr. H. Myles, the Representative of the

CUNARD LINE

AT THE PREMISES OF

FRANK SPEER,
MAIN STREET,
AUGHNACLOY,

ON

WEDNESDAY, JANUARY 13, 1926,

BETWEEN

11 a.m. and 5 p.m.

CUNARD LINE TO CANADA.

C2523.

Your opportunity *is in*

CANADA.

FAMILIES WANTED.

ASSISTED PASSAGES FOR

HOUSEHOLD WORKERS.

GUARANTEED EMPLOYMENT,
WAGES: £5 TO £8 PER MONTH.

FREE PASSAGES FOR BOYS UNDER 19.

SPECIAL OCEAN FARE
FOR BRITISH SETTLERS **£10** IRRESPECTIVE OF OCCUPATION.

ALL WHO ARE INTERESTED ARE INVITED TO CALL
FOR PERSONAL INTERVIEW WITH

ANCHOR-DONALDSON
REPRESENTATIVE

AT

Mr. Patrick Speer,
AUGHNACLOY,
On Wednesday, 6th Nov.,
FROM 12 NOON TILL 5 P.M.

Plate 6: *Emigration agents'/shipping lines' handbills advertising for emigrants to Canada, 1920s.*
(PRONI ref D.2607)

ronto, Ontario, giving family and political news and thanking Samuel for the receipt of money he has sent home.
T.3423/1/1-3

Letter, 5 June 1933, from William J. Stewart, Belfast, to Stewart Young, Regina, Saskatchewan, concerning genealogical information.
T.3423/1/4

75 letters, 4 July 1776-17 September 1788; from the 2nd Earl of Buckinghamshire, Lord Lieutenant of Ireland, 1776-80, to his brother-in-law, Sir Charles Hotham Thompson, [England]. The letters are sent from various addresses in England and Ireland and include many references to the war in North America. Particular comment is made on the effects of the war's actions on the Newfoundland fisheries.
T.3429/1/1-75

Letter, 19 July 1834, from James Robb, Coleraine, Co. Londonderry, to William Creighton, Thompkins Co., New York, mentioning that a Billy Park has emigrated to British North America.
T.3452

Although included in the Donoughmore archive this body of papers relates to Field Marshal Earl Ligonier, Commander-in-Chief in Great Britain, 1757-66, and Master-General of the Ordnance, 1759-63. He played a prominent role in the preparation for, and the conduct and conclusion of, the Seven Years' War but the material of particular relevance to Canada is limited. It includes:

Letter, 10 August 1762, from Colonel Amherst to Mr C. Fox informing him that he has just been appointed to command a body of troops to dislodge the enemy from their new acquisition of the island of Newfoundland.
T.3459/A/63

Report, 20 September 1762, by Hugh Devvieg, Ensign, St John's, Newfoundland, to Lieutenant-Colonel Amherst, entitled 'A report of the state and condition of the works at St John's fort in Newfoundland, before it was in possession of the enemy, and of the improvements and additional works done by them during their stay in that place'.
T.3459/A/64

Copy, 14 April 1763, of Lord Ligonier's representation to the Crown for a peerage and suggesting that if he had not been in charge of the Ordnance then Louisburg and Quebec might not have been taken.
T.3459/A/73

Report, [1763?], indicating the forces which had to be maintained in 1749 and upon what establishment. Alongside this are presented the figures for the necessary reductions to bring the current force to the same numbers and establishment in America. Also provided is an estimation of the rate of half pay at the conclusion of the war.
T.3459/A/75

Publication, 1980, entitled *Documents in the History of the Orange Order, Ontario and the West, 1890-1940* by R.S. Pennefather. Also included are lists of general errata and supplements to these; indices to prefaces and documents found in the pamphlet; and three copies of a newssheet regarding the acquisition of these.
T.3495/1-6

37 letters, 1882-1905, from Ernest Cochrane of Belfast, Dublin, Calgary, Alberta, and Regina, Sackatchewan, to Miss K. Finlay, Holywood, Co. Down. The first first letters deal with his time in the Royal Irish Constabulary and thereafter he writes from Canada, first as a member of the Royal Canadian Mounted Police and then as an employee of the Canadian Pacific Railway Police. Life and conditions in both forces are well documented.
T.3504/1/7-43

Letter, 1824, from James Humphrey, Highland Creek, York, Upper Canada, to his family in Coagh, Co. Tyrone, in which he describes the voyage to Canada, his journey to York and the price of goods and the rate of wages he found there.
T.3534/2

Petition, 4 April 1820, of William Portt and five of his sons, farmers of Hamilton, Ontario, to the Administrator of the Government of Upper Canada, requesting land. Portt had emigrated from Ireland seven months earlier, possibly from the Shannon area.
T.3566

List, 1848-9, of immigrants who received support and assistance from the Emigrants' Hospital of St John, New Brunswick, recording the name and age of those admitted, their disability, length of stay, name of ship in which they arrived, port of departure and place and date of disembarkation.
T.3568

Typescript reminiscences, 1909-70, of H. Bailey, who was born in Limerick, describing his life in the theatre and the circus, including a period in Canada. The permission of the donor must be obtained to gain access to the archive.
T.3581

Typescript Duncan family history, compiled in 1962 by Edward G. Burnside, Toronto, Ontario, giving details of those members of the family who emigrated to Canada from Ireland.

Typescript Davis family history, compiled in 1962 by Edward G. Burnside, Toronto, Ontario, with details of those members of the family who originated in Co. Leitrim and who emigrated to Canada, together with personal information as to where they left, where they went to in Canada and their subsequent progress.

Three letters, 1874-81, two of which are from Noble Beatty, Derrylonan, Co. Fermanagh, and from William R. Beatty, New York, to their half brothers, Thomas and James Burnside, California and Ontario. Also one letter from Anthony Kennedy, U.S.A., to Thomas Burnside. They cover mainly family news.
T.3594

Letter, 9 October 1910, from Robert Moffat, North Bay, Ontario, to his brother in Belfast about his work on the railway. He reports that another brother who works with him has been injured and has had a leg amputated.
T.3595/1

Letter, 5 April 1847, from James Calwell, Bellahill [*sic* Ballyhill], Ballycarry, Carrickfergus, Co. Antrim, to his cousin Mary Jane Calwell, Kingston, Ontario, referring to having received news of her birth and a subsequent lapse in correspondence. He gives her a list of her Irish relatives and their occupations and asks for news of her.
T.3614/1

Two letters, 2 June 1839-20 August 1846, from Hugh and Elizabeth Barkley, Killycoogan, Co. Antrim, to Hugh's sister, Ann, and her husband, Adam Stewart, Elmsley township, Smith's Falls, Upper Canada, referring to family news and to the possibility that there may be a famine in Ireland.
T.3616/1/1-2

Rent and tithe receipts, 1832-52, of Adam Stewart, Tamlaght, Co. Antrim, and South Elmsley, Smith's Falls, Upper Canada, where he emigrated to in 1834.
T.3616/2/1-14

Genealogical notes, c.1778-c.1950, compiled in 1982 and relating to the Stewart and Barkley families of the Portglenone area, Co. Antrim, and Upper Canada.
T.3616/3/1

Letter, 8 May-1 July 1858 from John McCracken, Quebec, to his sister, Kate, [Ireland], enclosing an account of his voyage from Belfast to Quebec. 51 pages.
T.3621/3

Letter, 4 May 1850, from Marianne Gurd, Montreal, Quebec, to her sister Fanny Payne, Edgeworthstown, Co. Longford, describing her way of life and recommending Canada as an emigrant's destination.
T.3664

Correspondence, 1878-91, of Thomas McMullin, Caradore, Mount Brydges, Ontario, from his friends and family in Co. Sligo. These include news of both family and political events in Ireland. There is also a letter from J. Armstrong on Canadian House of Commons paper, dated 9 May 1891, thanking McMullin for his petition which will be presented if possible. The collection also contains two genealogical lists with details of Irish emigrants to Canada.
T.3694

Two letters, c.1928, between Mrs Kidd, Belfast, and B. Tedford, New Glasgow, Nova Scotia, concerning Tedford's reminiscences of his youth living on the Newtownards Road, Belfast and playing around Stormont Castle. Tedford family photographs are also included.
T.3702

Letter, 8 March 1840, from William Quinn, Crew townland, Co. Antrim, to Richard Dillon, Perwe Village, Clinton County, New York. He comments on the poverty in Ireland and asks for advice about emigrating to either the United States or Canada and gives details of others who have left Ireland for Canada. He refers in particular to '... ten miles of Upper Canada, inhabited by people from our country ...' and he gives the names of some of these.
T.3718

Letter, 1 January 1855, from Daniel Waide and his wife, Drumrankin, Craigs, Co. Antrim, to their son, Alexander, Ontario, noting that he has been away from Ireland for three years and requesting information about the farm he has bought. News is passed on to other emigrants from their families and news is requested of them in return.
T.3724

Publication, 1951, entitled *Irish Emigrants' Letters from Canada, 1839-70* and compiled by Edward Norman Carrothers, Belfast. This is comprised of the correspondence between Nathaniel and Joseph Carrothers of Westminster and London, Ontario, on the one hand, and their brother William of Lisbellaw, Co. Fermanagh, on the other. The subject matter is extensive and includes family news, and details of their acquisition of property, local development, prices,

military activity in 1839 and local religious and agricultural practices. They were enthusiastic about Canada and sent home news of other immigrants as well as advice to those considering emigration.
T.3734

Genealogical material and related correspondence, 1894-1976, of the Killen family, originally from Drumduff, Co. Donegal, some of whom emigrated to Ziska, near Gravenhurst, Ontario, in 1867. The papers include four typescript letters to members of the family in Canada from their relations in Ireland, giving family news (the Canadian addresses are not given). There is also a pedigree covering the period 1852-1976 and a typescript letter from Clifford B. Reid, Montreal, Quebec, to his cousin Mrs Wesley Brady, Greenwich, New South Wales, Australia, providing genealogical information about the Killen family.
T.3740/1/1-3, /2, /3 and /4

Various papers, 1804-1962, of and about Sir John and Lady Franklin. They include personal papers and references about the search for his remains. There is also subsequent Lefroy correspondence about Franklin, mainly with the Scott Polar Institute, Cambridge.
T.3746/L/33-37

Miscellaneous material, 1860-1975, concerning the Canadian branches of the Lefroy family. They include personal papers, correspondence and a collection of photographs. Perhaps the most interesting item is a file of letters, 1904-32, of Walter John Magrath Lefroy, founder and editor of the journal *Canada*. This contains correspondence with numerous Canadian politicians, journalists and businessmen. There is also a typescript memoir of R.P. Lefroy, 1961, describing his life in Gloucestershire and Canada.
T.3746/B/12, /M/10, 56, 66, /T/1-6 and /W/27

MICROFILMS

Ordnance Survey Memoirs, 1833-47. These parish memoirs were compiled to complement the six inch Ordnance Survey maps which were produced for all the counties of Ireland during these years. Their main topics of concern were the natural features of an area, the modern topography and the social economy. It is this third area which contains material on emigration from Ireland to Canada but it is not uniformly informative or comprehensive. Counties Londonderry and Antrim receive particular attention with emigrants' names, ages, addresses, religion and destination being given for some 50 parishes in these counties. There are also copies of letters from emigrants to their families at home. PRONI holds both microfilm copies and transcripts of the originals which are deposited in the Royal Irish Academy and the Ordnance Survey Office, Dublin. (Reels 1-275 cover the six northern counties and 276-318 cover the counties of Cavan, Donegal, Galway, Lietrim and Louth. See also T.2383).
MIC.6

Passenger books, 1826-67, of J. & J. Cooke, shipping agents, Londonderry. These are microfilm copies of D.2892 and correspond as follows;
MIC.13/Reel 1 - D.2892/1/2, 1850-57.
MIC.13/Reel 2 - D.2892/1/1, 1847-9. D.2892/2/2, 1826-34.
MIC.13/Reel 3 - D.2892/1/3, 1858-67.
MIC.13

Newspaper extracts, c.1758, containing adverts for emigrant ships. Titles include the *Belfast News Letter* and the *Londonderry Journal*.
MIC.19

Letter, 26 December 1841, from Rev J.L. McHenry, curate of Culdaff, Co. Donegal, to his mother, referring to the death of Miss Anne Elizabeth Young. Miss Young died in Canada where she was living on her brother's farm, 'Culdaff', Ontario.
MIC.25

Letter, 3 May 1857, from Joseph and Margaret Cleland, East Guillmybury, Upper New York State, to Margaret's parents, Mr and Mrs Barr, Burren, Ballynahinch, Co. Down, referring to their proximity to the Canadian border and giving details of a trip they made across it.
MIC.33

Poster, 26 July 1847, by John Wilkinson, 7 Chichester Quay, Belfast, and William McEwing, Commander of *The Chieftain* announcing the sailing of *The Chieftain* from Belfast to Quebec.
MIC.45/3/59

Extracts, May 1792-April 1793, from the *Gordon's Newry Chronicle* which includes details of ships travelling to North America from Newry, Co. Down.
MIC.56

Copies, 3 June 1772-14 December 1887, of issues of the *Londonderry Journal*, including details of ships travelling to North America and other miscellaneous material on emigration.
MIC.60/1-59

Correspondence and papers, 1886-95, of F.B. Hayes, Ottawa. There are some 250 documents relating to Hayes's efforts to raise funds for the Irish Land League and the Irish Parliamentary Party in Canada. There is a considerable amount of detail about his methods and the origins of the subscriptions. Copies of invitations and public notices concerning the Home Rule movement are included. Hayes's correspondents are mainly Irish representatives of the League and Party.
MIC.95

Out-letter book, 6 January 1837-27 March 1847, of John Cooke, later of J. & J. Cooke, shipping agents, Londonderry. This is a copy of D.2892/2/1.
MIC.112

Diary, 1910-24, of James Boyd, a merchant seaman who made many transatlantic voyages. During his career he served on the Lord and Head lines, sailing between Northern Ireland and Canada. The entries are short, simply documenting the progress of the voyages or changes in his terms of service, with only a little additional information being given on the places he visited.
MIC.126

Printed notice, c.1862, of John O'Hagan, emigration agent, Liverpool, England, stating the times of sailings to Canadian ports from various British ports, with a list of the provisions provided *en route*.
MIC.181/1/5A

Two volumes of passenger account books, 1868-1934, of William Dalzell & Sons, shipping agents, The Quay, Coleraine, Co. Londonderry. They include details of passages to Canada. The accounts are laid out under the particular voyage, with the name of the ship, the date of sailing, destination, passengers' names and their payments all being recorded.
MIC.203

One reel of microfilm of inventories and calendars of collections in the Department of Public Records and Archives, Toronto, Ontario.
MIC.205

56 reels of microfilm, 1880-1916, of British Cabinet records which include many references to Canada, including several proposals with regard to emigration from the British Isles to Canada. The calendar provides a detailed list of the material to be found on each reel.
MIC.219/1-56

18 British emigrant guides, 1819-70. These printed works were designed to offer advice to prospective emigrants to the United States and Canada. They were all written by British-born authors for British audiences. Some of them cite experiences of particular emigrants, often with the inclusion of copies of letters sent home. The microfilm has an introduction which gives details of the authors and summarizes their work.
MIC.247/1-2

Unlisted papers of Thomas Spring-Rice, later 1st Earl of Monteagle, 1833-53. They comprise some 300 documents and contain references to emigration from Ireland to North America and to Spring-Rice's involvement in various assisted emigration schemes. The originals are in the National Library, Dublin.
MIC.284

Letter, 19 October 1864, from W.J. Romaire, the Admiralty, Whitehall, London, to A.H. Layard, the Foreign Office, Whitehall, London, voicing concern at the United States' deployment of armed steamers on the Great Lakes.
MIC.320/4

Passenger lists, 1800-91, of ships arriving at: Philadelphia, Pennsylvania, Baltimore, Maryland, Boston, Massachusetts, and New York. Aside from details of the passengers and ships, reference is also made to the other cargoes carried and to ships arriving from Canadian ports, including St John, New Brunswick.
MIC.333/1-4

Six letters, 1 November 1860-28 August 1872, from William Johnston M.P., Ballykilbeg House, Lecale, Co. Down, to Benjamin Disraeli, London, concerning Orangeism in Canada. Johnston criticised the British Government's policy regarding the Orange Order in Canada and in 1872 he made a tour of the Dominion and received a warm welcome from the Orange Lodges there.
MIC.337/3/62, 63, 76-78

Naval Office shipping lists for New York, 1713-65. These lists were compiled by the naval officers in the colonies and include a wide range of information on the vessels which entered New York. These included Canadian ships and a summary is provided of the extent of commerce between New York and Canada.
MIC.390/1-3

Correspondence, 1816-46, of Jacob Harvey, an Irish merchant in New York. The bulk of the material consists of 129 letters from Harvey to Thomas Spring-Rice, Ireland, 1st Earl of Monteagle, in which Canadian-American relations are discussed and reference is also made to internal Canadian politics in the 1830s. There is also some correspondence with the 7th Earl of Carlisle, Chief Secretary of Ireland, 1835-41, who had met Harvey during a tour of Canada and the United States in 1841-2.
MIC.390/7

Diary, 1824-1908, of Henry Edward Price. Born in an Irish workhouse, Price was sent to the United States under the Poor Law emigration scheme and there are several passing references to Canada.
MIC.390/10

Correspondence, 1884-1932, of Sir Horace Plunkett. Plunkett was actively involved in encouraging agricultural co-operation and he was President of the Frontier Land and Cattle Company of Wyoming. He acted as an intermediary between the United States and British Governments and whilst most of his correspondence deals with American affairs there are some references to Canadian matters.
MIC.390/11-12

Thesis, 1929, by Kathleen A. Walpole and entitled *Emigration to British North America under the early Passenger Acts*. It contains details of the operation of the Acts' provisions.
MIC.390/13

Scrapbook and working notes, 1673-1927, relating to the history of Co. Monaghan compiled by D.C. Rushe. They contain reminiscences of 'J.M.' of Toronto, Ontario, about his life in Monaghan before he emigrated.
MIC.426/1

Unlisted material, 1833-58, including newspaper cuttings, legal documents, photographs and emigrant letters of the Graham family, Keady and Newtownhamilton, Co. Armagh, and Hamilton, Ontario. There are some ten emigrant letters from Grahams who went to Canada. They describe their various fortunes and complain of the lack of assistance received from relatives already settled in Hamilton. There is also some correspondence from Grahams who moved on to Ohio.
MIC.446

Seven files, 1880-1921, of the Immigration Branch, Department of the Interior, Canada, which contain reports of the work of emigration agents in Ireland who were encouraging emigration to Canada. The topics covered include the appointment, payment and dismissal of the agents and their handling of anti-emigration propaganda, including that which claimed that the Canadian Government was unfriendly towards Irish Catholics. Copies of anti-emigration posters are also provided.
MIC.450/1-7

Two registers, December 1773-April 1776, of weekly returns of emigrants sailing from English ports. These include details of emigrants whose original residence was in Ireland and whose destinations included Canada. The information given includes names, addresses, ages, occupations, ports of departure, destination and the reason for going. Canadian destinations include Newfoundland, Quebec and Halifax, Nova Scotia.
MIC.462/1-2

CHURCH RECORDS

CHURCH OF IRELAND: DIOCESAN RECORDS

Metropolitan communications of a purely formal nature announcing to the Archbishops of Armagh the election and consecration of prelates throughout the world. These include notification of Canadian appointments, 1883-1934. The file is partially closed to the public. (Only 1-170 are open. The Canadian material is as follows DIO.4/3/1/2, 7, 20, 22, 29, 40, 51, 57, 58, 61, 68, 77-82, 87, 88, 97-99, 107, 114, 116, 117, 126, 134, 144, 145, 150-153, 155, 156, 160, 165.)
DIO.4/3/1/1-251

ROMAN CATHOLIC CHURCH: DIOCESAN RECORDS

Series of notebooks and notes, c.1800, handwritten in French, which formed a course in science, philosophy and theology, probably taught by the Abbé Louis Delahogue at St Patrick's College,

Maynooth, Co. Kildare. The material of Canadian interest includes a seven page notebook about the United States with information about the state boundaries of Ohio and Louisiana. There is also a one page note about Canada describing the geographical conditions and mentioning the principal rivers and towns.
DIO.(RC) 1/2E/3, 4

Letter, 1 April 1852, from Rev. Baile, President of the Sulpician seminary, Montreal, Quebec, to Charles McNally, Bishop of Clogher, Ireland, concerning two emigrants from Ireland who were studying at the college in Montreal. In French.
DIO.(RC) 1/10B/49

Diaries, October 1852-June 1855, kept by Dr James Donnelly, later Bishop of Clogher, describing his fund-raising tours for the Roman Catholic Church in Ireland in the United States and Canada. He visited Montreal, Niagara, Ottawa and Halifax. The daily entries include colourful descriptions of the people and customs he encountered. He also provides a list of Clogher men who were resident in North America.
DIO.(RC) 1/11B/2

PRESBYTERIAN CHURCH

Session book, 1842-50, of 1st Antrim Presbyterian Church, Antrim, which contains a register of certificates given to members 'leaving the congregation'. Some were issued to emigrants bound for Quebec. The information includes the date of issue, recipient's name and address and their destination.
CR.3/2A/2

Session minute book, 1835-68, of 2nd Dunboe Presbyterian Church, Co. Londonderry, containing a list of communicants' certificates, and including details of those issued to emigrants to Canada.
MIC.1P/149A/1

Baptism register, 1843-1985, of Gortin Presbyterian Church, Co. Tyrone. Entries up to the 1870s record details of emigration from the congregation. In some cases the Canadian destinations and the ships' names are provided.
MIC.1P/253A/1

REFORMED PRESBYTERIAN CHURCH

Minute book, May 1811-July 1825, of the Reformed Presbytery Synod of Ireland. It includes copies of letters to and from the Reformed Presbytery in North America and there are references to the administration of the church in the New World and requests of assistance from the Old.
CR.5/5A/1/3

List, 1842-92, of members of the Reformed Presbyterian Church, Fountain St, Londonderry. The personal details include the members names and their dates of baptism and of admission to communion. The names and dates of departure for families who emigrated are also provided and their destinations included Quebec.
CR.5/13E/1

SOCIETY OF FRIENDS

Register, 1838-1921, of Brookfield School, Moira, Co. Down, an agricultural training school for the children of those who attended the Society of Friends meetings for worship but were not

members. It contains the names of the children, their ages, addresses, the names of their parents, date of entrance and leaving, including those who emigrated to Canadian destinations.
CR.8/3/1

2. <u>LINENHALL LIBRARY</u>

The Linenhall Library, (Belfast Library and Society for Promoting Knowledge), Donegall Square North, Belfast, contains a fine representative collection of works on almost every subject, with some 50,000 volumes on open access and a total stock of some 200,000 volumes. The general index contains a large Canadian Section listing many printed works. However, this index is not, at the time of writing, up to date. More reliable indices are those concerning the Genealogical, Irish History and Northern Ireland Political Collections and they include the following references.

Genealogical collection

Buchanan, A.W.P.: *The Buchanan Book: the life of Alexander Buchanan, Q.C., of Montreal, followed by an account of the Buchanan family.* Printed privately, Montreal, 1911. Ref. **929.2 BUCH.**

A chronicle of the Dignam family, being a record of the descendants (and their spouses) of Hugh Dignam, who came in 1839, from Ireland to Upper Canada. Printed privately, Toronto, 1962. Ref. **929.2 DIGN.**

Covington, W.J.: *The Torontonian Society Blue Book and Club Membership Register: the social register, 1934.* Toronto, 1934. Ref. **929.54 COVI.**

Davin, N.F.: *The Irishman in Canada.* London, 1877. Ref. **929.6 DAVI.**

Hanna, C.A.: *The Scotch-Irish or the Scot in North America, North Britain and North Ireland.* Vol. 1. London, 1902. Ref. **929.6 HANN.**

Carrothers, E.N.: *Irish Emigrants' Letters from Canada, 1839-70.* Belfast, 1951. Ref. **929.6 IRIS.**

Royal Book of Crests of Great Britain and Ireland, Dominion of Canada, India and Australasia, derived from best authorities and family records. Vols 1-2. London, 1883. Ref. **929.82 MACV.**

Irish History Collection

Notices of the death of the late Lord Sydenham by the Press of British North America, with prefatory remarks. Toronto, 1841. Ref. Pam. no. **N/217.**

Bull, W.P.: *From the Boyne to Brampton or John the Orangeman at home and abroad.* Toronto, 1936. Ref. **N12588.**

Denison, F.C.: *Record of the Governor-General's Bodyguard and its Standing orders.* Toronto, 1876. Ref. **N15662.**

Irish Political Collection

This extensive collection relates to the current political troubles in Northern Ireland and the papers of Canadian interest are indicative of the contemporary links which exists between various political groupings in Northern Ireland and those who are sympathetic to their standpoint in Canada. They include:

Republican Publications- North America

3 newsletters, December 1985, March 1986 and September 1986, of the Irish Freedom Association, Box 596, Station U., Toronto. The president of the Association is Denis Laffan and a biographical sketch of Gerry Adams, the Sinn Fein President, is included alongside protests against the Canadian government's refusal to allow Adams to enter their country.

Newsletters and Press releases, 1981-7, of the Irish Prisoner of War Committee, Vancouver. They include protests during the hunger strike campaign in Northern Ireland and details of the visit to Canada of Jackie Donnelly, Sinn Fein's Press Officer, in October 1987.
Leaflet, undated, produced by the Irish Prisoner of War Committee, Box 5085, Station E., Hamilton, Ontario and entitled 'The British Army's Secret Opinion'.

Newsletter, 1982, produced by the Irish Prisoner of War Committee, Calgary and entitled *The Freedom Lark*.

Poster, 7 July [?], produced by the Irish Unity Information Service, P.O. Box 561, Pickering, Ontario, advertising Gerry Adams's visit to St Paul's United church.

6 newsletters, 1980s, of the Canadian Friends of Ireland, South Barnaby, British Columbia. They include instructions on how to write to the hunger strikers in Northern Ireland.

Copy of article (in French), December 1988, published in *L'Actualitie* entitled 'L'Agonie de l'Ulster' by Andrew Phillips.

Letters, posters and pamphlets, 1980s, produced by the Comité Quebec Irlande, Montreal. They document the activities of the republican movement in Western Ireland and there are references to the visit of Bernadette Devlin McAliskey to Montreal.

Unionist Publications - North America

Newsletter, 1974, produced by the Canadian Ulster Loyalist Association and entitled *The Canadian Ulsterman*. This is Vol. 1, no. 6 and it includes a list of donations made to the Niagara Committee in 1974.

In addition to these indexed collections there are other uncatalogued holdings. The references which I have been able to establish as having a Canadian import are given below, but it is unlikely that this is an exhaustive list.

Uncatalogued Irish Biography

Nasmith, G.G.: *Timothy Eaton*. Toronto, 1923.

Printed copy of the Memorial Service to Timothy Eaton held in St Paul's Methodist church, Toronto, on Sunday 10 February 1907. It includes an extract from the sermon and Press reaction to the death.

Lyall, A.: *The life of the Marquis of Dufferin and Ava*. London, 1905.

Milton, H.: *Speeches and Addresses of the Right Honourable, Frederick Temple Hamilton, Earl of Dufferin*. London, 1882.

Morgan, H.J.: *Sketches of Celebrated Canadians*. London, 1862.

Dufferin and Ava, The Marchioness of: *My Canadian Journal*. London, 1891.

Stewart, G.: *Canada under the Administration of the Earl of Dufferin*. Toronto, 1879.

Dufferin and Ava, Marquess of: *Journal of His Excellency, the Governor General of Canada, from Government House, Ottawa to British Columbia and back*. London, 1877. 23 copies.

Uncatalogued Orange Order pamphlets

Annual reports of the Grand Lodge of New Brunswick for the years 1876, 1886-8, 1896 and 1924.

Annual reports of the Grand Lodge of Central Canada for the years 1860-68. Also included is an Orange Directory of Central Canada for 1865.

Annual reports for the Grand Lodge of the Province of Ontario East for the years 1869-82.

Copy of dispatches sent from Sir George Arthur relating to Orange Lodges in Canada since 17 May 1837 and printed by the British House of Commons, 17 August 1839.

Uncatalogued Ulster Societies files

File, 1975- present, containing the quarterly journal of the Confederation of Ulster Societies entitled *Causeway*. It includes some details of the activities of Ulster Societies in Canada.

3. **MAIN LIBRARY, QUEEN'S UNIVERSITY, BELFAST**

Situated on the main campus, this library has a large and well catalogued collection of printed works concerning Canada. Whilst these would all be generally available there are some holdings which would be of particular use to researchers. These include the most extensive collection of British Government and Parliamentary papers in the Province. There is also a complete collection of all the Canadian censuses which have been gathered, along with a wide variety of Canadian legal material, including statutes and Case Reports. Queen's Main Library has only been a depository library since 1987 and although it does now receive Canadian Government publications these only cover this more recent period.

4. **BELFAST CENTRAL LIBRARY**

The Central Library, Royal Avenue, Belfast has a large and well catalogued collection of printed works concerning Canada. These would all be generally available and the library holds no manuscript collections in this area. It does, however, have an excellent collection of Irish periodicals containing articles on Canada and these are listed below.

Canada: The Canadas and emigration: an article based on '*Hints on emigration to Upper Canada especially addressed to the lower orders of Great Britain and Ireland*' by Martin Doyle: and '*The emigration guide to Upper and Lower Canada*' by Francis Evans. (*Dublin University Magazine*, Vol. 1, pp 287-303, March, 1833).

Magrath, T.W.: Letters from Canada: a review of *Authentic letters from Upper Canada* by T.W. Magrath. Etchings by Samuel Lover. (*Dublin University Magazine*, Vol. 1, pp 600-11, May, 1833).

Canada (a record of the coming of self-government). (*Dublin University Magazine*, Vol. 1, pp 326-53, March, 1838).

Prospects of the British Empire- Russia- Canada- Lord Durham- Governor Arthur's proclamation- dissent- establishment. (*Dublin University Magazine*, Vol. 13, pp 3-25, Jan., 1839).

Canada- Lord Durham's report. (*Dublin University Magazine*, Vol. 13, pp 356-68, March, 1839).

Canada: dispatches of Sir Francis Head: being a review of *A Narrative* by Sir Francis B. Head. (*Dublin University Magazine*, Vol. 13, pp 501-19, April, 1839).

Murray, H.: British America- the Edinburgh Cabinet Library, being a review of *A Historical and Descriptive Account of British America* (*Dublin University Magazine*, Vol. 15, pp 93-112, Jan., 1840).

Canada. (*Dublin University Magazine*, Vol. 20, pp 735-52, Dec., 1842).

The Canadas- how long can we hold them ? A review of *The Conquest of Canada* by a Canadian Loyalist. (*Dublin University Magazine*, Vol. 34, pp 314-30, Sept., 1849).

Canada. (*Dublin University Magazine*, Vol. 35, pp 151-68, Feb., 1850).

United States of America: The line of the Lakes. (*Dublin University Magazine*, Vol. 38, pp 159-77, Aug., 1851).

Rail in Canada. (*Dublin University Magazine*, Vol. 46, pp 127-37, Aug., 1855)

Hudson's Bay Company. (*Dublin University Magazine*, Vol. 51, pp 430-37, April, 1858).

Salmon Fishing in the Canadian River Moisie. (*Dublin University Magazine*, Vol. 58, pp 423-31, Oct., 1861).

England and her colonies. (*Dublin University Magazine*, Vol. 64, pp 482-96, Nov., 1864).

Dublin International Exhibition, 1865. Canadian exhibits. (*The Dublin Builder*, Vol. 7, no. 124, p 56, Feb., 1865).

Gildea, J.N.: The Dominion of Canada as a better field for the emigrant than the U.S.A., (*The Irish Builder*, Vol. 17, no.373, p 181, July 1, 1875).

Atthill, E.: Ancient pottery, found on the shore of Sturgeon Lake, Canada. (*Royal Historical and Archaelogical Association of Ireland Journal*, Ser. 4, Vol. 5, Pt 3, p 500, 1881).

Fisher, J.R.: Abstract of paper on Canada in the twentieth Century. (*Belfast Natural History and Philosophical Society Proceedings*, pp 1-4, 1909).

Dwerryhouse, A.R.: Abstract of paper entitled 'With the British Association in Canada in 1909'. (*Belfast Naturalists' Field Club Proceedings*, Ser. 2, Vol. 6, pt 3, pp 302-5, 1910).

Hunter, W.; Abstract of paper from Montreal to Victoria: an impression of Canada. (*Belfast Natural History and Philosophical Society Proceedings*, pp 15-16, 1912).

Bourke, M.J.: The early life of George Washington. With maps of the British colonies in America and northern New France, 1750-60. (*Cork Hist. and Arch. Society Journal*, Ser. 2, Vol. 29, pp 1-14, 1924).

Somerville, H.: Canada 1641-1941. (*Studies*, Vol. 30, pp. 173-82, June, 1941)

McF., R.: Review of *Phases in English Poetry* by Herbert Read, of *Other Canadians: an anthology of the new poetry in Canada, 1940-46*, ed. by John Sutherland, and of *Poetry Ireland* ed. by David Marcus. (*Rann*, No. 8, Spring, 1950).

Daly, C.: Pax Romana in Canada. (*Cork University Record*, no. 26, Christmas, 1952).

Duffy, D.: The success of Alphonse Desjardines. (*Irish Monthly*, Vol. 80, pp 392-7, Dec., 1952).

Rogers, H.C.B.: Reply to a query relating to Irish connections with Louis Riel's rebellion in Canada in 1870. Reply also by R. Hayes to the same. (*The Irish Sword*, Vol. 2, no. 6, pp 153-4, Summer, 1955).

Hunter, N.: North America, 1962. (*Acorn*, no. 4, Spring, 1963).

Noonan, G.R.: General John O'Neill, (who led the attempted Fenian invasions of Canada in 1866, 1870, 1871). With photograph. (*Clougher Record*, Vol. 6, no. 2, pp 277-319, 1967).

O Cathaoir, B.: American Fenianism and Canada, 1865-1871. (*The Irish Sword*, Vol. 8, no. 31, pp. 77-87, winter, 1967).

Duggan, G.C.: The Fenians in Canada, a British officer's (C.C. Grant) impressions. (*The Irish Sword*, Vol. 8, no. 31, pp 88-91, Winter, 1967).

De Valera, E.: President de Valera's official visit to the United States of America and Canada, 26th May to the 3rd June, 1964. Illustrated. (*The Capuchin Annual*, pp 182-197, 1965).

Lyne, D.C.: Irish-Canadian financial contributions to the Home Rule movement in the 1890s. (*Studia Hibernica*, no. 7, pp 182-206, 1967).

5. **THE ULSTER AMERICAN FOLK PARK**

The Ulster American Folk Park, Mellon Road, Omagh, Co. Tyrone, has set up a computerised database of historical records relating to Irish emigration to North America between the 17th and early 20th centuries. The original records are deposited in various archives throughout Northern Ireland, including PRONI and the Linenhall, Central and Queen's University libraries. This project has drawn all the relevant material together and made transcripts and, in some cases, high quality images of the documents so that they are now more readily accessible through the use of computer systems to researchers and visitors to the Folk Park. The information contained in this emigration database is readily available to academics, educationalists, school children, genealogists and members of the public. There are numerous references to Canada but the majority of these can of course be found in this catalogue. However, as the compilation of this database is spread over a much longer time span and as it is continuing after the completion of this catalogue, it is possible that some new material on Canada may be discovered.

6. **DOWNPATRICK MUSEUM**

This local museum, devoted to the documenting of the history of Co. Down, resides in the old

County Gaol in Downpatrick. The holdings of Canadian interest include a copy of the

Carrother's correspondence (*see* PRONI T.3734) and a printed pamphlet entitled *Fallona-Kelly*

c.1750-1983 by Marguerite M. Fallona, 1983. She traces the genealogy of these related families

from their arrival in Canada in the 1830s, with background information on their life in Ireland

before emigrating. The pamphlet includes photographs of both the Irish and Canadian home-

steads.

7. <u>**NEWRY AND MOURNE ARTS CENTRE**</u>

Situated in Newry town this small local museum has one item of Canadian import. This is a poster advertising the sailing of the ship *Lady Caroline*, captained by J. Malony, for New Brunswick on 4 June 1847. The local agent was Francis Carvill of Sugar Island, Newry.

Plate 7:   *Painted wooden mask Haida or Northern Kwaikuitl tribes, Northwest Coast.*
   (Londonderry Corporation 103: 1952)

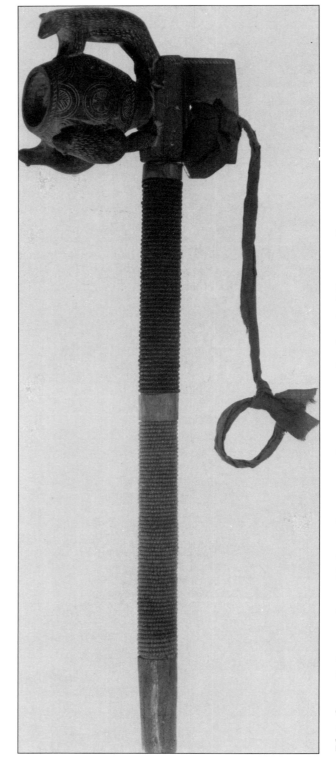

Plate 8: *Tobacco pipe with bear, beaver and otter supporting bowl: Micmac tribe of St John, New Brunswick.*
(1910: 153)

8. **NORTHERN IRELAND NEWSPAPERS AND CANADA**

In 1979 the first edition of a catalogue of newspapers produced in Northern Ireland since 1737 was published by the Library Association (Northern Ireland Branch)/ PRONI Working Party on Resources for Local Studies. *Northern Ireland Newspapers 1737-1987: a checklist with locations* was updated in 1987 and it forms a comprehensive checklist of the newspapers of Northern Ireland, listing the major collections of hardcopy editions in Northern Ireland repositories. Many of the titles included are now available on microfilm. There are some 235 titles listed and in many cases these include material relevant to Canada. They cover a broad spectrum; province-wide and local papers; daily and weekly editions; and from 1737 to the present. Similarly they cover a wide range of Ulster-Canadian links; political news; advertisements placed by shipowners and by emigration agents; articles on the extent and effects of emigration; and much more of interest.

This catalogue can be found in most libraries and in PRONI. It is also available from the Ulster Folk and Transport Museum, Cultra Manor, Holywood, Co. Down.

9. <u>ULSTER FOLK AND TRANSPORT MUSEUM</u>

This Museum, at Cultra, Co. Down, is devoted to the representation of late 19th and early 20th century Ulster; the Ulster which many of the Irish emigrants to Canada left behind. It contains a widely acclaimed collection of original buildings, reconstructing a cross-section of an Ulster landscape. The earliest of these dates to 1700 but the majority of the buildings, and all the furnishings, are from the turn of the century.

The Museum also houses an extensive reference library where both the catalogue of accessions and the index of manuscripts and printed works can be found.

Catalogue of Accessions

This contains thousands of entries but as it only classifies holdings by the nature of the artefact, and as there is no indexed guide to the origin of these artefacts, there is no simple or efficient method to check which holdings have a Canadian import. Furthermore, only some 40% of the holdings are actually catalogued. Thus little more can be said than that it is probable that there is relevant artefact material within the Museum, particularly in the collections of agricultural machinery and textiles.

Catalogue of Manuscript and Printed Materials

This is a more comprehensive index, including a separate Canadian section. However, it contains only one item of significance:

'A Student Preacher's Romance: A True Life Story', by J.D. Stuart. This autobiographical sketch is a mixture of typescript and freehand. Written post-1914, it includes some 40,000 words and begins in December 1909 when Stuart entered a ministerial training college in Vancouver. He describes life in the college and his apprenticehip as a student minister in the Squamish valley and the North-West prairies, where he was a nomadic preacher. He describes the Indians who still roamed the prairies before he was moved to Caribou Landing, where he taught Chinese immigrants and met other Irish Canadians. It was here that he met his sweetheart, Elva Lindner, daughter of Swiss immigrants. Elva died in a canoeing accident whilst Stuart was working at Arrow Lakes, Kootenay. Thereafter Stuart lived with his father who had settled in the Frazer valley until he left Canada to fight in the 1st World War. It is at this point that the autobiography ends. The narrative is punctuated throughout with poetry and has strong religious overtones, combining to provide a vivid and very personal account of one man's Canadian experience.

10. **ULSTER MUSEUM**

Situated in Botanic Gardens, Belfast, several of this Museum's departments have material relevant to Canada.

Art Department

A catalogue by Hugh Dixon concerning the work of the Belfast architect, William Henry Lynn (1829-1915), describes a Canadian connection. Lynn travelled to Canada in 1875 at the behest of the Governor General, Lord Dufferin. He designed the Chateau St Louis on the Heights of Abraham at Quebec and the terraces for which the city is now famous. Lynn made pencil and ink drawings and water colour sketches of the Chateau. He also made water colour sketches of three views of Niagara Falls in the same year. The Ulster Museum does not hold the originals but they do have photographic copies.

Botany Department

This department has two collections of Canadian plants, one catalogued and the other not. The first of these was assembled by Dr David Walker, a Belfast born surgeon/naturalist/photographer who accompanied the Fox expedition of 1859. This expedition was one of the voyages sent to the Canadian Arctic to search for the lost Franklin-Crozier expedition of 1845. Walker collected specimens in the following localities: Disco Island

> Port Kennedy
>
> Bellot Strait
>
> Cape Osborne
>
> Fiskemaer
>
> Pond's Bay
>
> Frederikshaab
>
> Cape York

Walker lectured to the Belfast Natural History and Philosophical Society on his return and his lecture was reproduced in the Society's journal on 7 December 1859, entitled *Notes on the Arctic Region*.

The second uncatalogued collection was made by two botanists from Queen's University, Belfast, Miss M.P.H. Kertland and Dr M.E. Morrison, in the 1960s.

Geology Department

The pertinent collection here was assembled by John Grainger, a Lisburn-born amateur naturalist, historian and geologist. In the autumn of 1858 he travelled to North America on a business trip, visiting New York, Niagara, Montreal and Quebec. He collected fossils, minerals, fresh water shells and butterflies and made notes on the geological formations he observed. This collection now resides in the Ulster Museum and the Geology department can supply a detailed list of its contents. An obituary notice for Grainger, who was ordained in 1863, appears in the *Annual Reports and Proceedings of the Belfast Naturalists' Field Club*, (1891-2), Series 2, Vol. 3, Part 5, pp 424-34.

Ethnography Department

The Museum's most important Canadian collections are to be found in this department and include both Inuit and Indian artefacts collected by travellers from Ulster to Canada.

The vast majority of the North American Indian artefacts in the Ulster Museum were collected by the Ulsterman, Gordon Augustus Thomson, (1799-1886) in a lifetime spent travelling the four continents in search of rare and important specimens from the native cultures he encountered. The Ulster Museum has produced a catalogue of their complete holdings of North American Indian artefacts, entitled *The Land of the Brave*, and the entries relating to Canada are reproduced here with the same regional distinctions.

The Northwest Coast

1. Bow (1.29m) and Arrow (92cm)

Shaped composite bow of wood strengthened with twisted gut and strip of bone. The bowstring is of twisted fibre. The arrow is of wood with a detachable four-barbed head made of bone and three-feathered nock. **Thomson Coll. 1910: 736**

2. Cradle (65cm)

Strongly-made boat-shaped carrying cradle in imbricated basket work. The sides are decorated with black and cream red dyed cane and the carrying straps of leather are fastened to the sides in four places. Thomson-Frazer River tribes. **A. MacDonald. 1939: 274**

3. Gambling sticks

Set of twenty-one gambling sticks from the Northwest coast, each one marked differently with painted bands. **Thomson Coll. 1916:32**

4. Harpoon (17cm) and Sheath

Ground slate harpoon head in barbed bone holder. The wooden sheath is bound with gut. This specimen is much older than the 19th century as very similar articles to this were being made when Cook brought back examples from his third voyage. Probably made by Nootka of Vancouver Island. **Thomson Coll. 1910:644**

5. Halibut Hooks (35cm)

Wooden hooks with fibre bound hook with iron barb. One is carved in the shape of a squid with two bird's heads inset, the other is carved in the shape of a sculpin. **Thomson Coll. 1911:1174**

6. Frontlet (22cm hgt, 29cm wdth)

Wooden frontlet of hawk gripping the head of a beaver. There are holes along the top for feathers, now missing. The two portions at the side are of leather. It is made all in one piece except for the claws which are of separate plugs of wood. One is loose and has been wedged in with a piece of gut. It is inset with abalone shell, some of which is missing. The hawk is pale blue with red lips and black eyebrows while the beaver is green with red lips and black eyebrows. Probably Tsimshian tribe. **Thomson Coll. 1910:60**

7. Mask (25 cm)

Painted wooden mask in blue and black with red lips, nostrils and chequered red ears. Masks such as these were worn by secret dancing societies at which the male dancer acted the hero of legends. The ends of the fibre mouthpiece can just be seen under the nostrils. Probably Tsimshian tribe. **Londonderry Corporation 103:1952**

8. Dagger (57cm)

Double-bladed copper fighting dagger with grip in centre bound with leather. Leather sheath and sling belt. The label states 'made by Indians from local copper'. **Thomson Coll. 1910:522**

9. Spruce Root Hat (41 cm diam)

Hat made from twined spruce root and painted with totemic bird and eye decoration in red, black and blue. An interior woven band fits the wearer's head and the inside of the crown is strengthened with a circle of wood set on. Haida. **Thomson Coll. 1910:264**

10. Spruce Root Hat (27 cm diam)

Twined spruce root hat showing European style influence. The Indian tribes were quick to imitate European styles which resulted in the woven cap illustrated. Possibly Haida. **Thomson Coll. 1910:266**

11. Grease Dish (20.5 cm)

Square kerfed cedar wood box in shape of a beaver holding a stick in his paws. The inlay around the rim and the beaver's teeth have been created by using nut kernels. This grease dish would have been used at feasts for holding grease or oil. The most common oil was that obtained from eulachon or candle fish. **Thomson Coll. 1910:65**

12. Food Dish (17.5 cm)

Oval dish of wood in the form of a beaver holding a stick between his incisor teeth and his front paws. **Thomson Coll. 1910:67**

13. Horn Dish (27 cm)

Dish in form of hollowed-out water bird with incised ornament on inside rim. Probably much earlier in date than 1830 since the modelling of the bird is early and there is much wear on the sides of the dish. **Thomson Coll. 1910:100**

14. Box (30 cm)

Square kerfed, bent wood box with deep relief carving of hawk's head at either end, its wings emerging from the sides. Cowrie shell inset around the rim. Haida. **Thomson Coll. 1910:66**

15. Leggings (42 cm wide)

One pair of cream coloured, dressed leather leggings with black and red painted decoration, which includes a bear's head and 'eye' motif. The tops are folded over and both they and the bottom edge are fringed. Probably worn on ceremonial occasions. Tlingit. **Thomson Coll. 1910:231**

16. Rattle (28 cm)

Painted wooden rattle depicting kingfisher, shaman and the mythical thunderbird which was supposed to cause thunder and lightning. Rattles such as these would have been used on ceremonial occasions. Probably mid-18th century in date. Haida. **Thomson Coll. 1910:3**

17. Shield (39 cm diam)

Painted wooden shield with wooden strip carrying handle. Remains of hair tufts around the edge. The decoration consists of black 'eye' motifs and orange claws on a green background. The animal represented may be a wolf. Probably used as a dance shield as it is only about 2 cm. thick. Kwakiutl. **Thomson Coll. 1910:735**

18. Needle Cases (11.5 cm, 14 cm)

Bone tubes with incised totemic decoration. The bases are filled in with pieces of wood and each has leather carrying ties. **Thomson Coll. 1925:2**

19. Hair Ornament (11 cm)

Ornament of blue beads and dentalium shell on leather backing with leather tie. Worn by the women folk of the Northwest Coast. **Thomson Coll. 1910:321**

20. Spoons (18.5 cm, 25 cm)

Two horned spoons, each with carved handles. The larger has an unfinished grotesque human figure and animal decoration while the smaller has a handle formed of a sea monster with shell inlaid eyes and arrow of shell inlay down the centre of the bowl. **Thomson Coll. 1910:111 and 112**

21. Spear Thrower (35 cm)

Carved wooden spear thrower with 'eye' decoration and a sea monster with protruding tongue. The atlatl or spear thrower was in use in North America from prehistoric times before the introduction of the bow and arrow. **Thomson Coll. 1910:735**

22. Pipe (11.5 cm)

Argillite pipe carved with elaborately intertwined composition of birds and men. The predominant bird is the raven whose head has a stylised human head inset. This part forms the bowl while the mouth piece is a stylised human figure clutched by a bird. Haida. **Londonderry Corporation 104:1952**

23. Pipe (29.5 cm)

Argillite pipe depicting two men, the waves of the sea and ropes. It is meant to represent European sailors who must have been a common sight to the Haida Indians of the 19th century. **Thomson Coll. 1910:161**

24. Rattle Basket (15.5 cm diam.)

Brightly coloured twined spruce root basket with symbols in false embroidery. This covered example has small stones contained in its hollow handle to provide a pleasing sound when used. Tlingit tribe. **C40:1977.**

25. Harpoon (1.23 m)

Fishing spear or harpoon with wooden shaft and bone socket at one end. The head is five barbed and attached by a long cord to the shaft. A seal-gut bladder to act as a float is attached to the shaft. **Thomson Coll. 1910:716**

26. Walrus Ivory Ornament (24 cm)

Ivory ornament composed of a row of small fish with the head and tail of a whale linked to each end. Two large seals hang down in the middle. Details are incised in black and the opercula of shells have been inserted for eye and tail decoration. This may have been used to embellish the clothing of a shaman. This ornament is almost certainly of Alaskan Eskimo manufacture but it is included here as there is no doubt where it was collected. Nootka Sound, Vancouver Island. **Thomson Coll. 1910:339**

Sub Arctic

27. Shirt

Shirt of soft deerskin decorated with a band of woven quill ribbon of orange and white round the shoulders, each strand of the fringe bound with quill, threaded through a dried nut kernel and tipped with orange dye. **Thomson Coll. 1910:204**

28. Jacket

Skin jacket with attached mittens, bordered with interlaced bands of coloured leather strips and edged with blue, white and black beads. **101:1917**

29. Hunting Bag (48 cm wide)

Bag of woven babiche with deerskin border, decorated with dyed quills and beads, the mesh ornamented with wool and deerskin tassles. Made by Indians at Fort Good Hope, Mackenzie River, 1898. **C41:1977**

30. Bag (28 cm)

Oval black cloth bag, trimmed with navy and beautifully decorated in ornate floral patterns with white, blue, pink, green and transparent beads. A small beaded handle of red and white beads is attached to the top. Fort Good Hope, Mackenzie River, 1898. **C42:1977**

31. Pouch (101 cm)

Pouch made from whole otter skin, its neck and paws bound with orange, white and blue woven quill ribbon while orange and blue moose hair tassles bound with metal trade jingles adorn its back.

Eastern Woodlands

(Some of these may not be of Canadian provenance)

32. Unfinished Mitten (19.5 cm)

Unfinished mitten of black dyed deerskin showing moose hair embroidery of the finest quality in ornate floral designs on the back, front and thumb. Possibly made as a trade object. Huron Indian. **Thomson Coll. 1910:291**

33. Birch Bark Boxes (22x18x16 cm, 15x13x10.5 cm)

Two rectangular birch bark boxes with closely fitting lids, one flat, the other domed. Both are richly ornamented with coloured quill embroidery in geometric designs. Micmac tribe, mid-19th century. **Grainger Coll. 1252 and 1254**

34. Pipe (25 cm)

Tobacco pipe with stone head carved with a bear, beaver and otter holding up the bowl. The wooden stem is bound with blue and green beads. Micmac tribe of St John, New Brunswick. **1910:153**

35. Moccasins (24 cm long)

Deerskin moccasins decorated with dyed moose hair tufting on instep and around the heel. The instep pattern is bordered by a band of pink, white and purple quill embroidery. Probably early 20th century. **H. Conn C43:1977**

36. Moccasins (24 cm long)

Deerskin moccasins with floral appliqué beadwork in red, green, orange, light and dark blue, bound with maroon and purple silk. Probably early 20th century. **H. Conn C28:1977**

37. Dish (15 cm diam.)

Delicate octagonal dish made of birch bark panels sewn together and embroidered with moose hair in floral designs of violet and white. Micmac. **1920:297**

38. Pipe Bag (90 cm)

Long soft leather deerskin bag with scalloped top trimmed with blue beads and with floral beaded panels in overlay beadwork of different design on either side. The long fringe is threaded with blue, white and metal beads. Late 19th century. **C44:1977**

39. Pouch (26 cm)

Deerskin pouch, beautifully ornamented with orange and cream quill embroidery. The strands of the fringe are bound with orange quill. **Grainger Coll. 1253**

40. Club (66 cm)

Characteristic woodlands weapon of ball-headed wooden club, the head surmounted by a carved animal, in this case a snake. **640:1954**

41. Pouch (25 cm)

Black cloth envelope style bag, bordered with green silk and richly embroidered in blue, white and green beads in ornate floral and scroll patterns. Woollen tassles hang from the bottom edge and the interior is lined with pinkish floral cotton. Said to have been made for Tuskina, Chief of the Creek Indians, by his daughter. **1910:271**

42. Birch Bark Container (22 cm)

Cylindrical bark container with stamped decoration, the top and bottom made from wooden roundels. Late 19th century. **Grainger Coll. 1297**

43. Cigar or Tobacco Box (10 cm)

Small rectangular birch bark container with sleeve lid. The borders are of lengths of white ash splints. The scenes on either side in moose hair embroidery depict seated and standing Indians smoking and one panel contains a bird perched on a bush. It contains a small roll of birch bark. **94:1962**

44. Sash (3 m)

Finger woven sash of wool. Such sashes were used for carrying small objects. This example is a very fine specimen. **Thomson Coll. 1910:232**

45. Model canoe (40 cm)

Canoe of wood and birch bark with quill embroidery. Birch bark canoes were constructed by sticking large strips of bark to wooden stakes.

Canoes of this type were made by both the Sub Arctic and Woodlands Indians. Micmac, late 19th century. **279:1920**

46. Lithograph (57 cm x 43 cm)

This hand painted lithograph is the work of Denis Dighton (1792-1827) who was appointed military draughtsman to the Prince of Wales in 1815 and made occasional trips abroad for his royal patron. In 1821 several lithographs, of which this is one, were published. The Woodlands Indians featured (probably Iroquois), practised face painting, wore ear-rings and nose ornaments and had tomahawks and pipes combined. Under each figure is the name with an English version beside it. From left to right the names read: Ne-gun-ne-au-goh (Beaver); Se-gous-ken-ace (I like her); Teki-cue-doga (Two Guns); Sta-cute (Steep Rock); Uc-tau-goh (Black Squirrel); Senung-gis (Long Horns, the Chief); Ne-gui-e-et-twafaaue (Little Bear). **C45:1977**

The Ulster Museum's Inuit holdings are both extensive and important. The 211 items are listed

below and it will be noticed that only a few have precise provenances and it would require a

great deal of research to attribute them to specific areas, but it seems likely that most of them

have a Canadian relevance. Once again, the Museum's own listings have been reproduced here.

INUIT COLLECTION

Dog Whip
Dog whip with wooden handle and rawhide lash.
C1:1989

Dog Whip
Dog whip with wooden handle and rawhide lash.
C2:1989

Dog Reins
Sealskin dog reins.
C3:1989

Dog Harness
Portion of dog harness made of leather and bone toggle.
C4:1989

Reins
Set of reins for dog sleigh
C5:1989

Reins
Set of reins for dog harness.
C6:1989

Sinew cord
C7:1989

Sinew cord
C8:1989

Sinew cord
C9:1989

Dog reins
Dog reins with bone toggle.
C10:1989

Dog Whip
Dog whip with bone handle. Probably part of the Hugh Conn Collection American Indian and Inuit specimens donated to the Museum in the 1950s. Conn worked for the Hudson Bay Company. Unfortunately no provenances were recorded for the material at the time.
C11:1989

Dog Whip
Dog whip with hide lash and bone handle.
C12:1989

Dog Whip
Dog whip with hide lash and bone handle.
C13:1989

Tea block
Russian tea block made of tea mixed with ox blood pressed into cake. Used by Inuit of Cape Serdze, Siberia. Donation J. A. Hunt.
775:1926

Dog whip
Sealskin whip used by Inuit dog driver. Ungra - N.E. Quebec approx. 1914. Donation J. F. Caldwell.
C14:1989

Rope
Rope made from sinew.
C15:1989

Basket
Rawhide basket with wooden rim. Cape Serdze, Siberia.
Donation J. A. Hunt.
776:1926

Reins
Reins for dog sleigh with two bone toggles. Probably Conn Coll..
C16:1989

Reins
Reins for dog sleigh
C17:1989

Caribou skin bag, (65 mm x 85 mm) Bag decorated with floral silk embroidery, Probably Conn Coll..
C18:1989

Bag, 65mm x 55mm
Caribou skin bag with fringe round edges and drawstring top. Floral silk embroidered decoration. Probably Conn Coll..
C19:1989

Waistcoat, (1000mm wdth, lgth 1200 mm)
White buckskin waistcoat with floral silk embroidery. Probably Conn Coll..
C20:1989

Coat
Man-sized smoked caribou skin coat heavily fringed and with ornate floral beadwork on front. Probably Conn Coll..
C21:1989

Coat
Caribou skin coat with floral silk embroidery. Probably Conn Coll..
C22:1989

Mittens
Mittens of felt with fur cuffs. Probably Conn Coll..
C23:1989

Gloves
Caribou skin gloves with wolverine fur trim. Cape Serdze, Siberia. Donation J. A. Hunt.
782:1926

Mittens
Set of mittens of felt with fur cuffs. Probably Conn Coll..
C24:1989

Moccasins, (lgth 250mm)
Caribou skin moccasins decorated with floral silk embroidery at ankles and vamp. Probably Conn Coll..
C25:1989

Moccasins, (lgth 230mm)
Unfinished moccasins. Probably Conn Coll..
C26:1989

Leggings
Leggings of cotton cloth with leather ties. Probably Conn Coll..
C27:1989

Moccasins, (lgth 200mm)
Child's moccasins of buckskin with silk embroidery. Probably Conn Coll..
C28:1989

Moccasins, (lgth 220mm)
Child's moccasins of buckskin with silk embroidery. Probably Conn Coll..
C29:1989

Moccasins, (lgth 245mm)
Buckskin moccasins with silk embroidery. Probably Conn Coll..
C30:1989

Moccasins, (lgth 87mm)
Child's moccasins of buckskin with silk embroidery. Probably Conn Coll..
C31:1989

Moccasin, (lgth 173mm)
Single moccasin of buckskin with silk embroidery. Probably Conn Coll..
C32:1989

Moccasin, (lgth 150mm)
Child's moccasin of buckskin with silk embroidery. Probably Conn Coll..
C33:1989

Moccasins
Baby moccasins of buckskin with silk embroidery. Probably Conn Coll..
C34:1989

Moccasins
Baby moccasins of buckskin with silk embroidery. Probably Conn Coll..
C35:1989

Moccasins
Baby moccasins of buckskin with silk embroidery. Probably Conn Coll..
C36:1989

Moccasins
Unsewn moccasins of smoked caribou skin with silk embroidery. Probably Conn Coll..
C37:1989

Mittens
Knitted wool mittens. Labrador.
263:1920

Dog Harness
Dog harness with bone toggle and walrus tusk attachment.
C38:1989

Slippers, (lgth 270mm)
Sealskin slippers with bead embroidery on toe. Donation J. A. Hunt. Cape Juneau, Alaska.
781:1926

Bow drill, (lgth 460mm)
Bone stave and hide string. **Grainger Coll..**
2351

Scraper, (lgth 300mm)
Iron bladed scraper with antler handle.
C39:1989

Pick, (lgth 310mm)
Antler with copper prong.
C40:1989

Fishing pick, (lgth 255mm)
Copper hook for hauling in fish. Copper, Eskimo, pre-1910.
C41:1989

Scraper
Hide scraper with stone head and wooden handle.
C41:1989

Ula, (lgth. 150mm)
Woman's hide scraper with bone handle and iron blade.
C43:1989

Toggles, (50mm)
Four ivory toggles.
C44:1989

Bow drill, (465mm)
Bow part of bow drill made of bone and hide.
C45:1989

Snow goggles
Wooden snow goggles. Ingalik Indian of Lower Yukon, possibly.
C46:1989

Figure, (lgth 54mm)
Tupilak figure, possibly. Donation J. A. Hunt.
778:1926

Figurine, (70mm)
Carved ivory figurine. Central Arctic.
C47:1989

Pipe bowl, (lgth 34mm)
Stone pipe bowl.
C48:1989

Snow knife, (lgth 285mm)
Snow knife made of antler.
C49:1989

Harness
Piece of dog harness with bone toggle.
C50:1989

Ice cutter, (lgth 222mm)
Ice cutter with bone handle and iron blade.
C51:1989

Rope
Piece of sealskin rope.
C52:1989

Harpoon model
Model harpoon with head, line and toggle comprised of leather, bone and metal.
C53:1989

Dog harness
Portion of dog harness with musk ox horn and walrus tooth toggle.
C54:1989

Knife, (handle lgth 155mm, blade lgth 276mm)
Knife with bone handle and copper blade.
C55:1989

Ivory chain
Portion of very old walrus ivory chain. Used in East and West Arctic. Donation J. A. Hunt.
785:1926

Snow goggles, (lgth 170mm)
Wooden snow goggles with hide ties. Probably Conn Coll..
C56:1989

Model harpoon, (lgth 61mm)
Model harpoon of wood with bone head. Probably Conn Coll..
C57:1989

Puffin beaks
Five puffin beaks perhaps to be used for rattle.
C58:1989

Needle case, (lgth 92mm)
Needle container without the needles. Ivory. DB752.
Donation Miss A. L. Price-Owen.
C59:1989

Harpoon head, (lgth 262mm)
Bone harpoon head.
C60:1989

Hook and line
Fishing hook of iron with bone and hide line.
C61:1989

Toy harpoon, (lgth 115mm)
Bone head and wooden shaft.
2408

Ivory carving, (lgth 34mm)
Ivory carving of probable bird.
C62:1989

Dog whip
Piece of plaited sinew thong for whip.
C63:1989

Scraper, (lgth 210mm)
Hide scraper with wooden handle and iron blade.
C64:1989

Fish hook, (lgth 112mm)
Iron fish hook with small lead weight and bone toggle.
C65:1989

Carvings
Small box of very small bone and wood carvings. Probably Conn Coll..
C66:1989

Ivory pendant, (lgth 27mm)
Walrus ivory pendant of smiling Buddha. Greenland. Donation J. A. Hunt.
777:1926

Seal pull, (lgth 85mm)
Seal pull of bone and sealskin. Netsilik pre-1910 in date.
C.67:1989

Bow tighteners, (lgth 114 mm)
Two bow sinew tighteners. Nineteenth century.
C68:1989

Marrow spatulae, (a) 176mm, (b) 200mm
Two spatulae for removing marrow from bones.
C69:1989

Snow beater, (lgth 870mm)
Snow beater of bone with copper rivet.
C70:1989

Snow beater, (lgth 800mm)
Bone snow beater.
C71:1989

Harpoon head, (lgth 219mm)
Walrus ivory harpoon head. St Lawrence Island, Alaska.
Donation J. A. Hunt.
769:1926

Knife, (lgth 291mm)
Knife and copper blade in hide sheath attached to belt with ivory belt hook. Cape Serdze,
Siberia. Donation J. A. Hunt.

Fish gorge, (lgth 42mm)
Fish gorge of bone and iron.
C72:1989

Model harpoon, (lgth 630mm, lgth of head 169mm)
Model harpoon with wooden shaft and bone head. Probably Conn Coll..
C73:1989

Model harpoon, (lgth. 484mm., lgth. of head 111mm)
Wooden shaft with detachable bone head. Probably Conn Coll..
C74:1989

Needle case
Sealskin piece with five bone needles stuck through it.
C75:1989

Fish gorge
Fish gorge of bone, iron with hide rope. Probably Conn Coll..
C76:1989

Toy harpoon, (lgth 252mm)
Wooden shaft and detachable bone head. Probably Conn Coll..
C77:1989

Fish gorge, (lgth 87mm)
Bone and iron fish gorge. Probabaly Conn Coll..
C78:1989

Harpoon head, (1gth 130mm)
Bone harpoon head with copper rivet. Probably Conn Coll..
C79:1989

Dog harness
Two portions of hide dog harness.
Grainger Coll. 3528

Bone toggle, (lgth 70mm)
C80:1989

Snow goggles
Wooden snow goggles minus ties.
C81:1989

Rattle
Puffin beak rattle, broken.
C82:1989

Bag
Canvas bag for holding fishing gear. Donation J. A. Hunt.
770:1926

Scraper, (lgth 212mm)
Hide scraper with musk ox horn handle, copper and iron blade.
C83:1989

Spear thrower, (lgth 408mm) Wooden spear thrower with small ivory peg and finer hole.
Aleutian Eskimo, rare and important. Donation J. von Stieglitz 1856.
1910:749

Blubber pounder, (lgth 322mm)
Musk ox horn blubber pounder.
C84:1989

Fish hook, (lgth 76mm)
Fish hook of bone and copper
C85:1989

Harpoon head, (lgth 89mm)
Harpoon head of bone and copper.
C86:1989

Snow scoop, (lgth 222mm)
Snow scoop of walrus tusk.
C87:1989

Fishing line
Fishing line with bone hook with metal barbs and a lead sinker. Cape Serdze, Siberia. Donation
J. A. Hunt.
770:1926

Hide cleaner, (lgth 150mm)
Hide cleaner of bone and iron.
C88:1989

Harpoon heads
Four iron harpoon heads.
C89:1989

Blubber pounder, (lgth 200mm)
Small blubber pounder of walrus tusk with finger ridges in handle.
Grainger Coll. 2390

Hide scraper, (lgth 273mm)
Walrus tusk handle set with steel blade.
C90:1989

Bow drill, (lgth 422mm)
Bow part of bow drill. Probably Conn Coll..
C91:1989

Skewers, (lgth 190mm)
Four bone skewers with sharpened ends.
Grainger Coll.. 1268

Knife, (lgth 142mm)
Metal blade and bone handle. Letters R.F. on handle.
C92:1989

Needle, (lgth 423mm)
Bone needle.
C93:1989

Walrus tusk.
C94:1989

Walrus tusk.
C95:1989

Plate 9:   *Wooden rattle depicting kingfisher, shaman and the mythical thunderbird: Haida tribe, Northwest Coast.*
(Thomson Coll. 1910: 3)

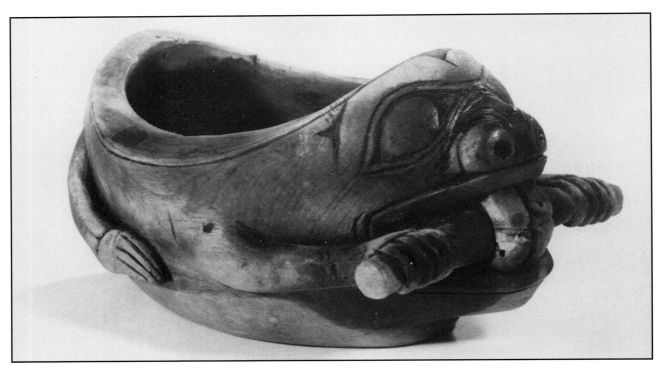

Plate 10: *Wooden dish in form of a beaver: Northwest Coast.*
(Thomson Coll. 1910: 67)

Bow drill, (lgth 400mm)
Bow part of drill. Antler stave and hide string.
C96:1989

Harpoons, (five ranging in lgth from 140mm to 273mm)
Harpoon heads of walrus ivory. St Lawrence Island, Alaska.
Donation J. A. Hunt.
769:1989

Knife, (lgth 327mm)
Iron blade set into bone handle and held in place by copper rivets.
C97:1989

Knife, (lgth 395mm)
Iron blade with bone handle.
C98:1989

Knife, (lgth 349mm)
Copper blade set in bone handle.
C99:1989

Pick, (lgth 5 mm)
Bone handle with iron spike held in place by copper rivets.
C100:1989

Implement, (lgth 5mm)
Ivory implement possibly a pipe head.
C101:1989

Implement, (lgth 66mm)
Bone implement possibly a knife handle.
C102:1989

Implement, (lgth 40mm)
Implement of copper and bone.
C103:1989

Implement, (lgth 43mm)
Implement of copper and bone.
C104:1989

Implement, (lgth 184mm)
Bone implement.
Grainger Coll.. 1268

Handle, (lgth 255mm)
Dog harness handle of walrus ivory.
C105:1989

Line
Piece of line of hide and sinew.
C106:1989

Implement, (lgth 521mm)
Bone implement with four pierced holes. May be arrow shaft straightener.
C107:1989

Dog harness
Part of dog harness, hide and bone.
C108:1989

Fish hook
Fish hook of iron set in bone and with sinew line.
C109:1989

Implement, (lgth 120mm)
Implement of walrus ivory with two grooves. St Lawrence Island, Alaska.
Donation J. A. Hunt.
767:1989

Beaks
Bunch of bird beaks.
C110:1989

File, (lgth 258mm)
File of iron set in wood handle.
C111:1989

Dog harness, (lgth 140mm)
Part of dog harness made of walrus ivory. St Lawrence Island, Alaska. Donation J. A. Hunt.
726:1989

Needle case, (lgth 139mm)
Part of broken bone needle case.
C112:1989

Bone skewer (lgth 232mm)
C113:1989

Harpoon head, (lgth 153mm)
Harpoon head of bone.
C114:1989

Ice pick, (lgth 300mm)
Ice pick with wooden handle, copper spike and hide thong.
Probably Conn Coll..
C115:1989

Ice pick, (lgth 289mm)
Bone handle set with iron spike.
C116:1989

Pick, (lgth 300mm)
Wooden handle with bone and copper head and hide loop. Probably Conn Coll..
C117:1989

Hook, (lgth 265mm)
Bone and iron hook.
C118:1989

Awl, (lgth 167mm)
Awl with wooden handle and iron spike.
C120:1989

Fishing spike, (lgth 116mm)
Bone handle with iron spike.
C121:1989

Peg, (lgth 180mm)
Walrus ivory peg.
C122:1989

Harpoon head, (lgth 141mm)
Harpoon head of bone.
C123:1989

Skewer, (lgth 179mm)
Skewer of sharpened bone.
C124:1989

Skewer, (lgth 146mm)
Skewer of sharpened bone.
C125:1989

Bodkin, (lgth 183mm)
Bodkin of walrus ivory. St Lawrence Island, Alaska.
Donation J. A. Hunt.
773:1926

Skewer, (lgth 172mm)
Skewer of sharpened bone.
C126:1989

Skewer, (lgth 130mm)
Skewer of sharpened bone.
C127:1989

Skewer, (lgth 130mm)
Skewer of sharpened bone.
C128:1989

Implement, (lgth 195mm)
Implement of walrus ivory.
C129:1989

Bone implement (lgth 160mm)
C130:1989

Bone implement (1gth 180mm)
C131:1989

Bone implement (1gth 180mm)
C132:1989

Needle case, (79mm lgth skewer, 117mm)
Needle case with bone skewer.
C133:1989

Model kayak, (lgth 701mm)
Model kayak with wooden frame covered with sealskin.
C134:1989

Model kayak, (lgth 458mm)
Wooden frame for kayak.
C135:1989

Model kayak, (lgth 635mm)
Model kayak of wooden frame covered with sealskin.
Greenland type.
C136:1989

Model kayak, (lgth 491mm)
Wooden frame covered with sealskin. Greenland type.
Grainger Coll.. 1284

Model sledge, (lgth 542mm)
Sledge of wood and sealskin with bone runners. East Arctic type
C137:1989

Model kayak, (lgth 735mm)
Model of wooden frame covered with sealskin
C138:1989 but may be Grainger Coll..

Model kayak, (lgth 531mm)
Wooden frame covered with sealskin.
Grainger Coll.. 1284

Model kayak, (lgth 610mm)
Model kayak with wooden frame and sealskin stretched over it.
C139:1989

Part of doll
Two legs and snow shoes, rest of figure missing.
Grainger Coll.. 1276

Model harpoon, (lgth 237mm)
Model harpoon with wooden shaft and bone and metal head.
C140:1989

Harpoon shafts, ((a) 222mm lgth (b) 230mm lgth)
Two harpoon shafts of wood and bone, minus heads. Probably Conn Coll..
C141:1989

Model harpoons, ((a) 260mm lgth (b) 252mm lgth)
Model harpoons of wood and bone.
C142:1989

Model harpoon, (lgth 264mm)
Model harpoon of wood and bone. Probably Conn Coll..
C143:1989

Model arrow, (lgth 280mm)
Model arrow with wood and bone shaft and copper head. Probably Conn Coll..
C144:1989

Model harpoons ((a) 120mm lgth (b) 116mm lgth)
Model harpoons of wood and bone. Probably Conn Coll..
C145:1989

Model harpoon, (lgth 290mm)
Model harpoon of wooden shaft with detachable bone head.
Probably Conn Coll..
C146:1989

Umiak model, (lgth 520mm)
Model umiak of sealskin stretched over wooden frame.
Probably Greenland type.
C147:1989

Model canoe, (lgth 511mm)
Model canoe containing figure and double-ended paddle tipped with bone.
C148:1989

Basket
Woven basket with green and brown decoration. Fort Wrangell, Alaska. de la Cour Carroll
Coll. c.1898.
C149:1989

Model harpoon, (lgth. 742mm, head lgth 260mm)
Model harpoon with detailed bone head.
Probably Conn Coll..
C150:1989

Scraper, (lgth 120mm)
Copper blade set in antler handle for scraping hides.
C151:1989

Model scoop, (lgth 214mm)
Model snow scoop of ox horn. Probably Conn Coll..
C152:1989

Model harpoon, (lgth 188mm)
Model harpoon of bone and wood. Probably Conn Coll..
C153:1989

Model arrow, (lgth 202mm)
Model arrow of wooden shaft with bone and copper head. Probably Conn Coll..
C154:1989

Paddles
Set of five model paddles, three broken.
C155:1989

Woman's costume
Greenland woman's summer costume of sealskin shorts with cotton gingham blouse trimmed
with sealskin and thigh-length red leather boots trimmed with sealskin. Donation by Commander Bingham O.B.E., R.N.
15:1950

Harpoon, (lgth. 1220mm, and lgth 424mm)
Full size harpoon with detachable bone head fitting into bone socket. Donation by Angus
McDonald.
C156:1989

Snowshoes, (lgth 1504mm)
Snowshoes of wooden frames with rawhide webbing and cloth ties. Probably Conn Coll..
C157:1989

Quiver, (lgth 801mm)
Rawhide quiver with decorated bone carrying strap and two bone toggles. Contains five arrows
with wooden shafts and copper heads. Probably Conn Coll..
C158:1989

Arrow
Arrow with wooden shaft and bone slot at end. Head missing.
C159:1989

Ice Beaters
Three ice beaters consisting of long pieces of polished bone.
C160:1989

Toy harpoon
Harpoon with wooden shaft and detachable bone head.
C161:1989

Knife
Knife with wooden handle in rawhide sheath.
C162:1989

Arrows (3)
(a) lgth 806mm, (b) lgth 801mm, (c) lgth 805mm,
4th arrow broken, (lgth. 535mm.) All have wooden shafts and copper heads and most of the
feather flights are missing. All probably Conn Coll..
C163:1989

Snow scoop, (lgth 1043mm)
Walrus tusk rim with whale bone netting. Cape Serdze, Siberia.
768:1926

Snowshoes, (lgth 625mm)
Wood frame with gut webbing and hide ties. Cape Serdze, Siberia, J.A. Hunt donation.
774:1926

Gauntlets
Smoked skin gauntlets with fur trim round wrist and top and heavily embroidered with floral designs on back of hand. May be Cree-Metis type. Probably Conn Coll..
C.164:1989

Composite bow, (lgth 1071mm)
Bow stave of whalebone with sealskin and gut binding. Copper rivets and repair with metal plate.
Grainger Coll. 2399

Composite bow, (lgth 1282mm)
Bow stave of shaped wood with strengtheners of bone and twisted sinew bindings. Twisted sinew bowstring. The stave has broken with the contraction of the bowstring but has been mended. This is a very good bow. The above bow should have had four arrows with it but at present only one remains, lgth 914mm with feathered nock, wooden shaft and detachable four-barbed bone head fitting into a short bone socket.
G. A. Thomson Coll. 1910: 736

Snowshoes, (lgth 975mm)
Wooden frame with rawhide webbing and ties of cotton cloth webbing. Probably Conn Coll..
C165:1989

Composite bow, (lgth 1087mm)
Bow stave of whalebone with metal, sealskin and twisted sinew strengtheners. Iron rivets hold the whole lot together.
Grainger Coll.. 2399

Snowshoes, (lgth 1010mm)
Wooden frames with rawhide webbing and leather ties.
Grainger Coll.. 1275

Snowshoes, (lgth 915mm)
Wooden frame with rawhide webbing, no ties. Probably Conn Coll..
C166:1989

Blanket or plaque, (wdth 1190mm)
Ornate blanket or plaque made for trading purposes by West Alaskan Inuit about 1898. It is made of the skins of the Arctic loon sewn together and backed with red flannel. It is a very handsome piece in white, grey and black.
C167:1989

Suit
Sealskin costume for small male. It may have been made by Inuit for wearing by a European because the front fastening of the trousers is untypical of Inuit manufacture at this time.
(a) jacket, lgth., including hood, 840mm.

(b) trousers, lgth. 990mm.
(c) 1 mitten, lgth. 255mm.
(d) boots, fine cream leather, hgt 495mm. These are summer boots in Greenland.
Donation by Dr J. Hill 1868.
1910:202

Drum, (diam. 610mm) and one drumstick of wood and cloth.
Drum of round wooden frame with handle over which is stretched a hide cover. This is a type
typical of Copper Inuit. Probably Conn Coll..
C168:1989

Aleutian helmet, (lgth 410mm)
Aleutian painted wooden helmet with strip of whalebone ending in a small seal's head at the top.
Streamers of sea lion whiskers protrude from the back and there are four Russian trade beads on
the front. These Aleutian pieces were collected in 1839 when Thomson was in Siska.
G. A. Thomson Coll. 1910:268

Model kayak, (lgth 458mm)
Wooden frame for kayak.
C135:1989

Model kayak, (lgth 635mm)
Model kayak of wooden frame covered with sealskin. Greenland type.
C136:1989

Model kayak, (lgth 491mm)
Wooden frame covered with sealskin. Greenland type.
Grainger Coll. 1284

Model sledge, (lgth 542mm)
Sledge of wood and sealskin with bone runners. East Arctic type.
C137:1989

Model kayak, (lgth 735mm)
Model of wooden frame covered with sealskin.
C138:1989 but may be Grainger Coll..

Aleutian wallet, (164mm x 108mm)
Woven wallet in blue, red, green and white for holding sewing equipment. Thomson said it was
made by a Russian woman in the settlement but it is a typical Aleutian type.
G. A. Thomson Coll.. 1910:314

Kayak ornament, (lgth 152mm)
Ivory ornament consisting of straight piece carved in small whales. At either end attached by a
link is the head and tail of a large whale. Suspended from the central portion are two representations of sea otters which were significant to the Aleutians.
G. A. Thomson Coll. 1910:339

Bolas
Eight oval shaped pieces of ivory attached to gut strings and held together at one end. For
ensnaring the legs of birds when hunting. Aleutian.
G. A. Thomson Coll. 1910:708

Needle case

Bone needle case with piece of hide attached through which are threaded copper needles. Ornamental top of Aleutian style. May be Thomson Coll..

C169:1989

Foster, John, 1st Baron Oriel, 11
Foster, Vere, 39
Fox, C, 61
Fox, H S, 26
Franklin, Lady Jane, 64
Franklin, Sir John, 44, 50, 64

Gage family, 34
Gage, Lt Col Connlly, 9
Gage, Rev. Robert, 45
Galbraith family, 53
Galbraith, Annie, 53-4
Galbraith, H, 54
Galbraith, William, 39
Galt, John, 36
Gamble family, 37
Gamble, James, 37
Gamble, Malcolm, 37
Gamble, Sarah, 37
Gamble, William, 37
Garbett, Cyril Forster, Archbishop of
     York, 27
Garrett family, 33
George III, 42
George IV, 92
George V, 12, 35
Germain, Lord George, *see* Sackville-
     Germain, Lord George
Gibson, Edward, 1st Baron
     Ashbourne, 56
Gibson, James, 17
Gibson, Peter, 37
Gildea, J N, 76
Gihon, Willie, 17
Gilmour, Sir John, 3
Gladstone, W E, 56
Glenelg, Lord, *see* Grant, Charles
Glenfield family, *see* Glinton/
     Glenfield family
Glinton/Glenfield family, 33
Gordon family, 56
Gordon, Richard Lewis, 56
Gordon, S S, 54
Gordon, Lt William E A, 56
Gosford, 2nd Earl of, *see* Acheson,
     Sir Archibald
Gowan, Miss P, 48
Graham family, 67
Graham, Campbell, 23

Graham, Sir James, 14
Graham, Ogilvy, 21
Graham, T Irvine, 32
Grainger, John, 85
Gransden, Sir Robert, 10
Grant, C C, 77
Grant, Charles, 1st Baron Glenelg,
     26
Granville, 1st Earl, *see* Carteret,
     John
Granville, 2nd Earl of, *see* Leveson-
     Gower, Granville George
Graves, Mrs Mercy, 40
Green, Professor E R R, 38, 49
Green, James, 47
Greeves, George F, 28
Greeves, Thomas, 12, 43
Grey, Sir Charles Edward, 26
Gribben, John, 48
Guest, Hon. Mrs Lionel, 20
Gurd, Marianne, 63

[H], Martha, 53
Haldane, Robert, 26
Hamilton, J B, 19
Hamilton, Eliza, 28
Hamilton, James Albert Edward,
     3rd Duke of Abercorn, 12
Hamilton, Mary Jane, 28
Hamilton, Robert, 28
Haney, E, 17
Hanlon family, 14
Hanlon, Edward, 14
Hanna family, 16, 37
Hanna, C A, 70
Hanna, Norman, 37
Harper, James, 31
Harvey, Jacob, 66
Harvey, Sir John, 26
Hastings, Francis Rawdon, 2nd
     Earl of Moira, 20
Haughton, Col S G, 5
Haviland, Col, 47
Hay, Anna, 20
Hay, Tom A, 18, 20
Hayes, F B, 65
Hayes, R, 77
Hazen, Moses, 43
Head, Sir Francis, 26, 75

McConnell, Jane, 57-8
McCracken, Kate, 63
McCracken, John, 63
McCrea, John Jnr, 26
McCrea, Master, 26
McCrea, Samuel, 23
McCreight family, 52
McCullough, Thomas, 58
McCurdy family, 32
McDermot, John, 60
McDermot, Mrs Margaret, 60
MacDonald, A, 86
McDonald, Angus, 106
MacDonald, Sir John, 15, 39
MacDonald, John A, 55
McDonnell, Randal John Somerled,
     8th Earl of Antrim, 40
McElderry, William, 49
McElhill, Thomas, 31
McEwing, William, 65
McF., R, 76
McGough, Alexander, 47
McGreer family, 32
McHenry, Rev. J L, 65
McHenry, Mrs, 65
McIlrath (née Wallace), Eleanor, 16
McIlroy, Miss Elsie, 35
McIlroy, S, 29
MacKay, William, 42
McKay, J, 30
McKean, Edward, 51
McKean, G, 51
McKee, Alexander, 45
McKee, F, 40
McKee, Robert, 45
McKee, Major W C, 5
Mackenzie, Alexander, 15
McKibben, Miss Ellen, 58
McKibben, Henry, 58
McKinney, William, 59
McMullan family, 63
McMullan, 'Aunt Elizabeth', 58
McMullan, Mary, *see* Price, Mary
McMullin family, 54
McMullin, Mrs Elizabeth, 54
McMullin, Thomas, 63
McNally, Charles, Bishop of
     Clogher, 68
McNeill, Dr Donald B, 25

McQuarters, John, 13
Macoun family, 32, 54
Magrath, T W, 75
Maguire, Susan, 28
Maitland, Sir Peregrine, 36
Malony, Captain John, 80
Marcus, David, 76
'Maria', 50
Marshall, Florence P, 28
Marshall, John, 31
Marshall, Margaret Ellen, 28
Marshall, R L, 31
Marshall, Rev. W F, 4, 31
Martin, Charles, 29
Martin, Ebeneezer, 29
'Mary', 17
Matthews family, 29
Matthews, Alexander, 29
Maxwell family, 40
Maxwell, Henry, 41
Maxwell, Col John, 19, 42
Maxwell, J W Jnr, 36
Mayne, Annie, 48
Mayne, Lowry, 48
Meade, Sir Robert Henry, 34
Meek, S, 52
Meighan family, 28
Melville, 1st Viscount, *see* Dundas,
     Henry
Meredith, Randal, 42
Middleton, Christopher, 40
Miller, Isaac, 17
Miller, John, 28
Miller, Miss, 28
Milton, H, 72
Minto, 4th Earl of, *see* Elliot, Gilbert
     John Murray Kynynmond
Mitchell, Captain William, 20
Mitchell, Mrs William, 20
Moffat family, 62
Moffat, Robert, 62
Moira, 2nd Earl of, *see* Hastings,
     Francis Rawdon
Montgomery family, 12, 16
Montgomery Hyde, Harford, 30
Montgomery, Matthew, 16
Montgomery, Richard, 42
Montgomery, Robert, 12
Montgomery, Robert H, 16

see under Clothing manufacture
and trade
Harbour Commissioners, *see under*
Ports and harbours
Harland & Wolff Ltd, *see under* Ships
and shipping
Heraldry, *see under* Peerage and
orders of chivalry
History, 85
Canadian, 72, 75
economic, 19, 53
Irish, 70, 77
local, 1, 22, 28, 31, 35, 39-40, 48, 51,
57-8, 64, 67, 75, 76-7, 81
see also Archaeology; *also* Armed
services; *also* Diaries, autobiographies
and biographies; *also* Economy; *also*
Philosophy and theology; *also* Science;
also Town planning and improvement
and urban development
Holiday resorts and spas, 28, 45
see also Sport and recreation
Home Rule, 53, 56, 77
anti-Home Rule Movement, 18
Home Rule League, *see under*
Political parties and parliamentary
groups
Hospitals, *see under* Medicine
Hotels, restaurants, and public
houses, 7, 11
Household and family, 18, 20, 26, 37-9,
43-9, 52, 54-6, 58-63, 65, 82-3
courtship and engagement, 5
legal papers, 12
marriage, 44-5, 57-8
orphans, female, 10
separation and divorce, 19, 51
see also Aboriginal and
tribal societies; *also* Emigration;
also Estate ownership and
management; *also* Poor Law
Houses of Assembly, of Commons,
see under Government
Hudson's Bay Co., *see under*
Manufactures, crafts and trades,
miscellaneous: fur and skin trade

Immigration, 19, 35, 37, 39, 47-8, 51,
53, 67, 83
Indian (American), *see under* Aboriginal
and tribal societies
Industrialists, *see under* Industry
(General)
Industry (General), 5, 7
see also Commerce; *also* Economy;
also Trade
Insects, *see under* Animals, birds and
insects
Insurance and friendly societies, 11, 30,
31, 36, 50, 60
see also Ships and shipping
International congresses, *see under*
Diplomacy and foreign relations
Inuit, *see under* Aboriginal and tribal
societies
Irish circuits, *see under* Legal system
Irish Land League, *see under* Political
parties and parliamentary groups
Irish Parliamentary party, *see under*
Political parties and parliamentary
groups
Irish Protestant Benevolent Society, *see*
under Orange Order and associated
bodies
Irish Unionist Alliance, *see under*
Political parties and parliamentary
groups

Jesuit Bill, 1889, *see under* Religion
Jewellers, and watch and clock busi-
nesses, 42, 88, 94, 97, 108
see also, Aboriginal and tribal
societies; *also* Dress
Journals, *see under* Diaries,
autobiographies and biographies

Labour, Russian, *see under* Employment
Lacrosse, *see under* Sport and recreation
Land agents, *see under* Estate ownership
and management
Land purchase and reform:
Antrim, Co., 15
Calgary, 33
Canada West, 52
Ireland, 44

Transport
Rebellions and insurrections:
  Canada:
      Declaration of Independence, 1869,
        16
      Fort Garry disturbances, 1874, 16
      rebellions, 21, 42, 44, 51, 63-4
      Riel's rebellion, 1870, 77
      Sioux rising, 1862, 55
Regiments, *see under* Armed services
Religion:
  General:
      Churches, 1, 10, 16, 29, 41, 53
      missions, 15-16, 20-22, 51, 54,
        57, 82-3
  In Ireland:
    Church of Ireland:
      bishops and clergy, 67
    Presbyterian Church in Ireland, 68,
    Protestants, 1, 10, 23, 85
    Reformed Presbyterian Church, 68
    Roman Catholic Church, 1, 17, 56,
      59, 67-8, 77
      bishops and clergy, 14, 42
      Capuchin Annual, 77
      education, 12, 67-8
      Orders, 12, 46
  Religion elsewhere:
    Anglican Church, 27
    Buddhism, 98
    Episcopal Church in Canada, 27,
      72
    Methodist Church in Canada, 72
    Presbyterian Church in Canada
      and America, 16, 21-2, 34, 57
    see also Aboriginal and tribal
    societies; *also* Diaries, autobiogra-
    phies and biographies; *also* Educa-
    tion; *also* Emigration; *also* News-
    papers and periodicals; *also* Phi-
    losophy and theology; *also* Poli-
    tics; *also* Taxation
Rent, *see under* Estate ownership and
  management
Repeal, *see* Union: Irish
Repealers, *see under* Political parties
  and parliamentary groups
Republicanism, *see under* Political
  violence and security (20th Cent.)

Revolutions:
  American Revolution, 4, 42, 43
  see also Rebellions and
  insurrections; *also* Wars and
  campaigns
Riots and disturbances, 17, 39
  see also Orange Order and
  associated bodies
Rituals, *see under* Aboriginal and tribal
  societies
Roads, *see under* Transport
Roman Catholic Church, *see under*
  Religion
Royal Canadian Mounted Police, *see*
  under Police
Royal Commissions and parliamentary
  committees, 15-16
Royal Irish Constabulary, *see under*
  Police
Rugby, *see under* Sport and recreation:
  football
Rum, *see under* Alcoholic drink

Schools, *see under* Education
Science:
  botany, 84-5
  geography, 68, 75
  geology, 54, 85
  natural history, 54, 76, 85
Scott Polar Institute, *see under*
  Education
Sea-monsters, *see under* Myths and
  legends
Seeds, *see under* Agriculture
Separation and divorce, *see under*
  Household and family
Seven Year's War, *see under* Wars and
  campaigns
Shields, *see under* Arms
Ship assurance, *see under* Insurance and
  friendly societies
Ships and shipping, 14, 15, 23, 29, 31,
    34, 57-9, 64-8
  Merchant Navy, British, 2
  Shipbuilding:
    Canada, 5, 31
    Ireland, 2, 9, 30
  Shipping agents, 11, 29, 30-31, 32, 45,